"Roberts and Wilson show how the exodus is more than a past event; it is a paradigm that shapes the storyline of the Bible and the life of the believer. The blend of rich biblical theology and beautiful writing will stir the affections of all who long for the Promised Land of the new heaven and new earth."

Matthew S. Harmon, Professor of New Testament Studies, Grace College and Theological Seminary

"Alastair Roberts and Andrew Wilson have written a marvelous book. In 176 packed, lucid pages, they explore the exodus, one of the Bible's main themes from Genesis to Revelation. The authors say that Scripture is musical, and their book will leave haunting echoes of exodus ringing in your soul. *Echoes of Exodus* won't just teach you about exodus; it will teach you how to read. In studying it, you will learn to harmonize on the melody of God."

Peter Leithart, President, Theopolis Institute; Contributing Editor, *Touchstone* Magazine

"I treasure books that bring the Scriptures to life, such as this one. This is what biblical theology should look like. This work by Roberts and Wilson taught me a great deal about the Bible and gave me a renewed appreciation for the exodus motif throughout God's Word. Seminary professors, preachers, Bible study leaders, and others are going to love *Echoes of Exodus*."

Mark Jones, Teaching Elder, Faith Vancouver Presbyterian Church

ECHOES OF EXODUS

ECHOES OF EXODUS

Tracing Themes of Redemption
through Scripture

Alastair Roberts and Andrew Wilson

WHEATON, ILLINOIS

Echoes of Exodus: Tracing Themes of Redemption through Scripture
Copyright © 2018 by Alastair Roberts and Andrew Wilson
Published by Crossway
   1300 Crescent Street
   Wheaton, Illinois 60187

Cover design: Jeff Miller, Faceout Studios

Cover image: Bridgeman Images

First printing 2018

Printed in the United States of America

Trade paperback ISBN: 978-1-4335-5798-9
Epub ISBN: 978-1-4335-5801-6
PDF ISBN: 978-1-4335-5799-6
Mobipocket ISBN: 978-1-4335-5800-9

Library of Congress Cataloging-in-Publication Data

Names: Roberts, Alastair, 1980– author.
Title: Echoes of Exodus : tracing themes of redemption through scripture / Alastair Roberts and Andrew Wilson.
Description: Wheaton : Crossway, 2018. | Includes bibliographical references and index.
Identifiers: LCCN 2017012930 (print) | LCCN 2017054810 (ebook) | ISBN 9781433557996 (pdf) | ISBN 9781433558009 (mobi) | ISBN 9781433558016 (epub) | ISBN 9781433557989 (tp)
Subjects: LCSH: Exodus, The—Typology. | Liberty—Biblical teaching. | Redemption—Biblical teaching. | Bible—Theology.
Classification: LCC BS680.E9 (ebook) | LCC BS680.E9 R625 2018 (print) | DDC 220.6/4—dc23
LC record available at https://lccn.loc.gov/2017012930

Crossway is a publishing ministry of Good News Publishers.

VP		28	27	26	25	24				
15	14	13	12	11	10	9	8	7	6	

For Derek Rishmawy and Matt Anderson

Contents

Acknowledgments 11

Prelude: Echoes of the Exodus 13

OVERTURE

1 A Musical Reading of Scripture 21

2 The First Supper (Matthew 26) 28

FIRST MOVEMENT: OUT OF THE HOUSE OF SLAVES

3 From the Bulrushes to the Bush (Exodus 1–3) 35

4 The Battle of the Gods (Exodus 4–15) 41

5 True Freedom (Exodus–Deuteronomy) 47

6 Journey's End (Joshua 1–7) 53

SECOND MOVEMENT: THE EXODUS IN GENESIS

7 People of Rest (Genesis 6–9) 61

8 Russian Dolls (Genesis 10–15) 65

9 Just Like Us (Genesis 16–26) 70

10 Wrestling with God (Genesis 27–50) 75

THIRD MOVEMENT: THE REECHOING OF EXODUS

11 Wings of Refuge (Ruth) 83

12 The Capture of God (1 Samuel 1–7) 88

13 All about the House (1 Samuel 15–2 Samuel 24) 93

14 The End of the Exodus? (1 Kings 6–13) 99

15 Elijah and Elisha (1 Kings 16–2 Kings 13) 104

16 The Outstretched Arm (Isaiah–Malachi) 109

17 Purim and Purity (Ezra–Esther) 116

FOURTH MOVEMENT: THE GREAT DELIVERANCE

18 The Crescendo (Matthew–John) 125

19 The Exodus of Jesus (Matthew–John) 131

20 Sinai and Pentecost (Acts) 137

21 Paul's Gospel (Romans–Jude) 142

22 The Exodus of Everything (Revelation) 149

Coda: Living the Exodus 155

Notes 160

General Index 165

Scripture Index 173

Acknowledgments

For a short book, this has been long in gestation. The seeds of this project were first sown in our thinking by scholars such as Tom Wright, Tom Holland, James Jordan, Peter Leithart, Greg Beale, and Richard Hays. They were supported in earlier stages of their growth by academic mentors such as Canon David Kennedy, encouraged towards fruitfulness by Bobby Jamieson and Justin Taylor, and wisely tended and pruned by Tara Davis, Amy Kruis, and the team at Crossway.

From their first germination to their full expression, they were nourished in the rich soil of friendship. In particular, we would like to thank Derek Rishmawy and Matthew Lee Anderson, our partners in crime on the Mere Fidelity podcast, for the blessing of their wisdom, friendship, and conversation over the past few years. It is to them that this book is dedicated.

Prelude

Echoes of the Exodus

The exodus is central to the Scriptures, central to the gospel, and central to the Christian life. Whatever book of the Bible you are reading, and whichever Christian practices you are involved in, echoes of the exodus are in there somewhere.

This is not the kind of thing you can establish through logical argument: *A*, therefore *B*, therefore *C*. Stories don't usually work that way. You can't prove logically that *West Side Story* is based on *Romeo and Juliet*. The echoes cannot be proved, any more than you can prove that a joke is funny. Rather, they have to be *heard*.

Our approach in this book starts from there. We hope to convince you that Scripture contains all sorts of connections, riffs, and themes that you may not have noticed, but we hope to do this by showing rather than by telling. Sometimes you may disagree. You may think we're reaching, or you may think we've missed something. In many ways, that doesn't matter. As long as we recognize that *The Lion King* is based on *Hamlet*, we can agree to disagree on whether Nala is an anti-Ophelia, or whether we can see Rosencrantz and Guildenstern in the characters of Pumbaa and Timon.

Having said that, we will generally err on the side of hearing those echoes more, rather than less.[1] Partly this is because we think those connections are actually there, both in the events themselves, through the providence of God, and in the ways the biblical writers have told their stories. Partly, though, it is because we can see a number of ways in which a greater appreciation of the unity of Scripture, especially when it comes to the theme of redemption from slavery, can help strengthen the church in the twenty-first century. Four ways in particular spring to mind.

One: much of the contemporary church, especially in evangelical circles, suffers from a rootlessness that makes it easy to lose our bearings, and even our identity. We live in a disoriented and rootless age.[2] Novelty and self-expression are prized above wisdom and experience. Inevitably, this has affected the church, not just in its forms of worship, but in its very sense of identity. In this sort of world, there is no better way of finding our moorings than reading the Old Testament (in particular) as if it were, as Paul puts it, "written for our sake" (1 Cor. 9:10; see also Rom. 15:4; 1 Cor. 10:11). We view the Scriptures, and the exodus in particular, as not just *their* story, but as *ours*. "Our fathers were all under the cloud," Paul tells the Corinthians (1 Cor. 10:1). They all passed through the sea. They all ate spiritual food and drank spiritual drink. And these things happened as examples *for us*, their great-great-etc.-grandchildren (vv. 1–6). We are to read about the exodus like we might read about the D-day landings: as a defining history that explains who we are. The exodus is our family story.

Two: the more we see the connections between the Testaments, the less likely we are to succumb to the idea that the God of the Old Testament is morally inferior to or must be distinguished from the God revealed in Jesus. Few people will explicitly state it like this, but many are eager to put as much distance as possible between, say, the conquest of Canaan and the person of Jesus, as if the latter could never have approved of, let alone commanded, the former. Others have gone further and argued that God simply never kills anybody for any reason, so every instance of violence in the Bible that implicates God should be seen as (a) incompatible with Jesus, and therefore (b) invented by ancient Israel.[3] Seeing the extent to which the exodus story is echoed throughout Scripture, not least in the ministry and teaching of Jesus, exposes the fragile foundations of all kinds of neo-Marcionism.[4]

Three: our generation is confused as to the nature of true freedom. No matter how often we experience liberation from constraints, limitations, and oppression, we still find ourselves falling into new forms of bondage. We get free from boredom, and fall into slavery to distraction. We pursue liberty from prohibitions, and fall into bondage to addictions. We escape repression, and become enslaved to lust. We are released from isolation, and fall captive to peer pressure and the power of the online mob. We pursue liberty from the constraints upon our natures, and fall into bondage to our untrained passions. We successfully break out of *1984*, only to find ourselves in *Brave New World*. Or, in the imagery of *The Hunger Games*, we get free from fences and guns in the districts, only to find ourselves trapped by slavish banality in the Capitol. True freedom is more complicated than it looks.

So, for example, the twenty-first-century church in the West faces two pressing ethical challenges that would seem to pull it in opposite directions. The first is the need for racial reconciliation and justice, which in the wider culture is generally seen as a progressive cause; the second is the need to remain orthodox on sexual ethics, which is typically a conservative concern. When framed in a secular way, these aims look to stand in tension: either you denounce your past prejudices and pursue radical inclusion for everyone, maximizing freedom by removing all constraints and limitations, or you stand firm in the face of

cultural pressure and preserve the traditions of your fathers, re-
stricting people's freedom for some higher cause. When framed
by the exodus story, however, these categories disintegrate. Our
redemption story is one in which "freedom *from*" is inextricably
bound up with "freedom *to*." God's people are exodus people,
so we know *both* the pain of oppression on racial grounds in
Egypt, *and* the dangers of compromise, idolatry, and immorality
in the wilderness. We also know that there is little point in being
free *from* serving Pharaoh if we are not also free *to* serve the
Lord. So we are not defined by the categories of 1789 or 1968,
by progressive and conservative, left and right. We pursue true
freedom—whether from Egypt or the golden calf, oppression or
immorality—knowing that if the Son sets us free, we will be free
indeed (John 8:36).

Four: for a variety of reasons, different sections of the church
today have become aligned with particular images, models, or
pictures of the atonement, leading to a shrinking of the biblical
gospel, as well as a fair bit of disunity and suspicion. (Some say
"I am of Christus Victor," some say "I am of reconciliation,"
some say "I am of penal substitution," and others say, "I am of
Christ.") Reactions have bred counterreactions, and the center
of our faith has, somewhat tragically, become a source of con-
tention.[5] The exodus story, however, because it is so long and
recurs so often, provides a wonderful framework for thinking
about how all the different atonement imagery fits together. It is
a story of redemption from slavery, involving blood sacrifice, a
substitute, liberation, reconciliation with God, a great victory,
vindication through faith, union with God, adoption, priesthood, Passover, baptism, kingdom, and probably others—all
of which, of course, also take place through the cross—and as
such, the exodus story helps us grasp how these many descriptions of what Christ has done for us can all be true, without
needing them to be played off against each other.

All of this is to say: we reap all sorts of benefits when we see the unity of Scripture, particularly when it comes to the exodus.[6] Nevertheless, most of this book is not about any of those things. In the main, it is a book about the exodus theme in the Bible, written to help people make more sense of Scripture, more sense of the gospel, and more sense of the Christian life. Our hope is that it will help fuel your prayers, your worship, and your joy, and that in seeing the exodus in a new light, you will see the God of the exodus in a new light as well.

OVERTURE

1

A Musical Reading
of Scripture

Scripture is music.

We use musical metaphors all the time when we talk about the Scriptures, without even thinking about it. We might describe the Bible as a *symphony* or a *love song*. We might refer to the opening of Genesis as an *overture* or to Revelation as a *finale*. We might talk about the story being *composed* or perhaps *orchestrated* by God, with *themes* and *rhythms* and *echoes* running through it, all building to a *crescendo*. If we are handling some of the difficult sections, we might say that there is a *clash* here or a *discordant note* there, but that there is always, ultimately, a *harmony* within the Word of God, and therefore that we can expect things to *resolve*. We could describe John as written in a different *key* than the other three Gospels, or Chronicles as a *transposed* version of Kings. We might even identify specific books with particular musical modes or styles: Job is the blues, Ecclesiastes is jazz, some of the psalms are in the minor key, or whatever. Much of our language for Scripture is musical.

That might sound trivial. After all, we use figures of speech all the time, and don't necessarily intend for them to be taken that seriously. But the reality is that metaphors, particularly ones that are applied consistently in a particular context, exercise a powerful influence over the way we conceptualize things, and this influence can be helpful, damaging, or neither. It's worth thinking about that for a moment.

To start with a fairly neutral example: we tend to understand people's theories and arguments in terms of buildings. This idea is *foundational* to my understanding. I *demolished* his case by *destabilizing* his assumptions. I *built* my argument and *supported* it with further examples. I *constructed* a defense for the position; the *structural weakness* of her theory can be seen at this point; their position was *shaky*; my view was *robust*; his argument *collapsed* under cross-examination. This controlling image isn't particularly harmful, and it isn't particularly illuminating, but it constrains our thinking more than we realize (as evidenced by the fact that all of us do it, and very few of us even notice). Metaphors matter.

Consider a different example, where the influence of the controlling metaphor might be more of a problem. Politicians use the language of war in all sorts of nonliteral settings. We have wars on terror, on poverty, on drugs, on obesity, on waste, and apparently on an ever-increasing number of abstract nouns. We must *fight* this, we are going to *defeat* that, the real *battlefield* is here, and so on. The war metaphor is familiar, and so it manages to relieve some of the sense of fear and discomfort we are experiencing (this *menace* is out there, and it is a genuine *threat*, but don't worry everyone, we will *conquer* this *enemy*). It also focuses the mind, implying an immediate and serious threat to our well-being as a society, and therefore the need to make the matter in question a top priority, even if it demands costly commitment and sacrifices. At the same time, the concept of war encourages us to think in very binary terms—good guys and bad guys, heroes and villains, enemies to be defeated and territory to be defended—which, when oversimplifying complex problems, has backfired in various ways in the war on terror and the war on drugs. It raises the rhetorical stakes and rallies people to a cause, but turns everyone into opponents or allies, when many are neither, or perhaps even both (a point which is made powerfully in movies like Steven Soderbergh's *Traffic* and Peter Berg's *The Kingdom*).

But now imagine that instead of employing military metaphors when speaking about a problem like, say, poverty, we employed a fabric metaphor instead. Say we talked about the *frayed edges* of society and recovering the *stitches* we once dropped. Say we lamented the *unraveling* of communities, addressed the *knotty tangles* of social problems, and argued that belonging to *close-knit* families was a crucial *thread* in the *fabric* of society. That metaphor might cause us to think and act rather differently. It would subtly teach us to think of our problems less in terms of opposition to an external enemy and more in terms of our interconnectedness and the importance of maintaining the integrity of society's relationships. It would alert us to the delicate character of social problems and of the need for patience, care, and measured action in addressing them, lest tangles become knots by being pulled too hard, or dropped stitches lead to unraveling by being ignored for too long. On the face of it, the only change would be our choice of metaphor—but the implications could be substantial.

The point is this: metaphors have great power to fashion the way we conceptualize things, even when we don't notice they are doing it. If a controlling metaphor is chosen well, it has the capacity to illuminate new worlds of meaning and help us see all sorts of connections we might otherwise have missed.

So it is with Scripture and music.

• • • •

A musical approach to Scripture encompasses a number of aspects, each of which can help us see Scripture in a fresh light. One, which we have already mentioned, involves the language of tension and resolution. Sometimes two or more books of the Bible, or even two or more parts of the same book, seem to clash with each other, and no resolution is obvious. Yet as the biblical piece develops, we find new themes being introduced, which bring the various instruments together, rearrange things somewhat, and resolve with a harmony that does justice to all of them. Sometimes the clashes are sustained and deliberate and uncomfortable to listen to, but they point forward to a future moment when things will be brought back together again by the master Composer. Scripture, in that sense, is true like jazz.

Another aspect of the music metaphor is the relationship between melody and harmony. The Bible has a clear storyline, a melody, a tune, and it can be summarized (or sung) by a small child. It also has a range of individual and corporate stories that run together, sometimes taking center stage, sometimes fading into the background, providing harmony and counterpoint, treble and bass, height and depth, in such a way that no single writer (or musician) could possibly represent it all. Like Beethoven's famous "Ode to Joy," the Bible is both memorably simple, even catchy, and incredibly intricate at the same time. Biblical study is about exploring the detail of the harmony— Why is the oboe, or Obadiah, doing *that*, and how does it contribute to the whole piece?—without losing sight of the melody. Biblical meditation is about listening to the music for enjoyment, not mere interest, to the point where we dance to its rhythms, sing its choruses, and whistle its melodies on the bus into work.

A third (and more subtle) aspect is the interplay between rhythm and meter. Meter is the underlying time structure of a piece, whether it is audible or not—*one*, two, three, four, *one*, two, three, four—and although it may vary within the piece, it provides a grounding in time, a sense of orientation, for the listener. Rhythm is the structure of the sound you actually hear—boom, ba-*cha*, boom, boom, ba-*cha*—which may involve a number of notes in one beat, or a number of beats without notes. The rhythm rides the meter like a surfer rides a wave, playing, doing its own thing, but always mindful of and constrained by the steady movement underneath.

Scripture works in a similar way. Chronologically speaking, every day is as long as every other day, with the passing of weeks, months, seasons, and years providing a meter for the piece as it unfolds. If we want to, we can form timelines from the Bible, reconstruct histories, and synchronize dates with external sources. But the rhythm of Scripture is not like that. Strong, accented, audible beats dominate the rhythm—Sabbath, Passover, the Day of Atonement, Pentecost, and the like—and they form regular patterns that draw repeated attention to particularly important moments in the story. And because the rhythm is repeated so much, every time we hear it, we are somehow transported back to the first time we heard it and forward to the next. So when Mary approaches the tomb early in the morning of the first day of the week, while it is still dark, we are swept back to the first day of the very first week, while it was still dark, and we anticipate the Word of God shattering the darkness: "Let there be light!" From then on, as the first day of the week becomes the Lord's Day, we look back to creation and back to Easter, and simultaneously look forward to the day when all darkness will become light, and death will be finally swallowed up in victory. Metrically speaking, all beats are equal. Rhythmically speaking, some beats are more equal than others.

When we bring these three aspects together—tension and resolution, melody and harmony, rhythm and meter—we get a full, rich picture of the connections between the different parts of Scripture. As the Bible commences with its overture, we hear a melody, and a regular rhythm begins. As things develop, various harmonies and counterpoints arise, some of which complement the melody beautifully, but some of which chafe against it, leaving us listeners to wonder what the Composer is doing. (Often, of course, we cause the dissonance, and he is simply waiting for the right time to heal it.) Then the melody returns, cutting through the cacophony and bringing a temporary sense of resolution. To someone who has never heard the piece before, it could even sound like it has been fully resolved and is about to finish (a new reader of the Bible could easily think the tension is resolved, for instance, upon the entrance into the Promised Land or David's coronation). Yet these temporary resolutions produce tensions of their own, which point forward to more complexities, and beyond them, to further resolutions. Throughout the Bible, as time metronomically marches on, the rhythms of Scripture continue to be accented, with particular days and festivals highlighting rest and freedom, law and atonement. But every bar, every cadence, every pause, heightens the sense that the piece is still incomplete. Eventually, after an uncomfortably long silence, the score builds to a massive crescendo in Christ, as the various themes come together and resolve in a fashion that nobody could have imagined, bringing the audience to its feet. Yet even then, the piece does not end but continues to develop themes and ideas, progressing toward a conclusion, echoing the original melody throughout, and retaining (while modifying) the original rhythms. Only at the finale, when the Christ-crescendo is recapitulated and the instruments are joined by earthly and angelic choirs, do we ultimately see the full scope of the Composer's vision.

As such, a musical reading of Scripture does more justice to the way Scripture actually works than, say, a pictorial reading, or even a dramatic reading. Plays are linear: this happens, then that happens, and although the past obviously shapes the present and future, it never comes back. Pictures are representative: this is a picture, an image, a copy, a shadow, a silhouette of that. Scriptural typology is more like a piece of music: familiar themes like temple, kingdom, exodus, judgment, and sacrifice keep recurring, but always slightly differently. The judgment of Jerusalem is not just a "picture" or "shadow" of the last day; nor is it simply a dramatic "event" that happens once and then is no more. It is somehow a part of the future judgment, a foretaste of it, and yet at the same time historically distinct from it. The final resolution, when it comes, is both familiar and new at the same time. It is, in that sense, musical.

• • • •

This all sounds a bit floaty and a bit abstract. In many ways, it is. In fact, it's the sort of approach to Scripture that is far easier to see than to imagine, and far more useful to show than to describe. We need to see this approach in action to fully get our heads around it. So that's what the rest of this book is going to try to do, using perhaps the clearest example of a recurring, time-condensing, rhythmic, melodic theme in the entire Bible— one that illuminates the opening pages of Genesis and the closing pages of Revelation, the whole history of Israel, the Gospels, the Letters, the Christian life, and of course the death and resurrection of Jesus.

The exodus.

2

The First Supper

Matthew 26

Meals can transcend time. Taste, and particularly smell, can evoke intense memories and take us immediately back to the last time we experienced the same flavor or aroma. Ritual meals, celebrated the same way with the same food, drink, and format every year, can connect the decades together in ways that nothing else does—so an American family celebrating Thanksgiving in 2017 is closer, in many ways, to Thanksgiving 1917 than it is to the previous Tuesday.[1] If we are looking to earth the "musical" nature of history in experienced reality, with the themes and echoes of previous movements heard afresh in the present, then meals are probably our best option.

God knows this. He created us this way. So on the night he rescued his people from Egypt, forming the identity of a nation that would last for thirty centuries and counting, he did it through a meal. According to Exodus 12–13, in fact, he spent a significant portion of that crucial day telling the people of Israel not just what to do, but how to memorialize it: what to eat, when to eat it, and what to say when their children asked about it. The story of the Passover, for all its drama, is told in a curiously liturgical way. From its inception, its music was intended to be performed, and heard, for thousands of years.

And it has been. Even today, the Passover seder is celebrated all over the world, with the same story being told, the same matzot (unleavened breads) and bitter herbs being eaten, the same cup of wine in the center of the table, the same songs being sung at each table. The constant, consistent repetition of this musical meal, despite exile and dispersion, pogrom and Holocaust, is at the heart of Judaism. And that makes it all the more remarkable that on a Thursday evening in Jerusalem, forty years before the destruction of the second temple, the most famous Jew of all summons the orchestra, brings the music to a crescendo, and rearranges the melody.

"Take this," he says, tearing the matzo into pieces and passing it around the table. "This is my body, which is given for you. Do this in remembrance of me" (Luke 22:17, 19). This alone is astonishing. Jesus is specifically identifying the unleavened bread as representing his body, which goes beyond the purity and unleavenedness of Israel, and he is telling his Jewish followers to celebrate the Passover in memory of *him*, not just their liberation from slavery in Egypt. After they have eaten, he takes the wine cup and goes one better. "Drink of it, all of you, for this is my blood of the covenant, which is poured out for many for the forgiveness of sins. I tell you I will not drink again of this fruit of the vine until that day when I drink it new with you in my Father's kingdom" (Matt. 26:27–29). This is not just a new understanding of Passover; it is a new covenant altogether. The kingdom of the Father is nearly here. Jesus's blood is going to move Israel's history from one phase to another. Sins are going to be forgiven and remembered no more, as the prophet Jeremiah said. The great deliverance is coming.

By saying these things in the context of a Passover meal, and by giving the events of the next twenty-four hours a memorializing, liturgical shape—just as the Lord had through Moses—Jesus is doing more than creating an analogy. He is not just saying that his death for them is a bit like the death of the Passover lamb for Israel, or that their liberation from sin is a bit like their liberation from Egypt. In taking these familiar symbols and investing them with new content, combining continuity and discontinuity, he is accenting the story of Passover in a different way and adding meaning to it that nobody had previously seen. It is not just that the Last Supper evokes the Passover in hindsight; it is that the Passover evokes the Last Supper in advance. Jesus's broken body and spilled blood, in some mysterious way, is bound up with the fact that Israel ate matzot and drank wine in the first place. The deliverance from slavery to Pharaoh was always going to be fulfilled in the deliverance from slavery to sin. The Mosaic covenant builds toward the new covenant. Passover culminates in Eucharist.

Within this Passover-shaped framework, with its rich array of images, the meaning of Christ's death comes into sharp focus. Passover is, if you like, the crucial clue that helps us decipher a much larger puzzle. Jesus is the firstborn Son, who dies in the climactic divine judgment under a darkened sky, opening up the doors of God's house. Jesus is the Passover Lamb, whose bones are preserved from being broken and whose blood proclaims freedom rather than condemnation. Jesus is the angel of the Lord who goes before us, forging a path through the deep, so that we might pass through on dry land. Jesus is the one who outwits and overcomes the great dragon in an almighty showdown, drowning Death in death at the very point when our Enemy presumes he has triumphed. Jesus is the Shepherd like Moses, who is struck but leads his people out. Jesus is the one who establishes a new covenant in his blood, sealed in a covenant meal that alludes to the covenant meal of Sinai (Ex. 24:11), and invites everyone to join him. Jesus is the pure, unleavened

Bread of Life, the Lord of the wine which symbolizes new creation, the one who eats the herbs of bitterness with us, and the one who explains to his descendants what all these symbols mean.

Yet even as he does all these things and is all these things, he is still pointing forward to the eschatological celebration to come. "I tell you I will not drink again of this fruit of the vine until that day when I drink it new with you in my Father's kingdom" (Matt. 26:29). The fact that Passover is *fulfilled* does not mean that it is *finished*. The Last Supper, like the First Supper, celebrates God's deliverance without regarding the story as complete, fanning the flames of hope as well as gratitude. One day, Jesus says, there will be new wine, a new kingdom, a new creation, and a new deliverance, and I will be with you forever. That day, as well as this one, is what you are looking to as long as you take the bread and drink the wine. But until it comes, do this in remembrance of me.

Review Questions

1. How can meals work musically?
2. Name three ways in which the Passover can illuminate the meaning of the death and resurrection of Christ.
3. What are some of the ways that the Last Supper looks forward to the future?

Thought Questions

1. Why might Jesus have chosen a meal as a primary framework for presenting the meaning of his death?
2. In Luke 22:16, Jesus declares that he "will not eat [the Passover] until it is fulfilled in the kingdom of God." How does the kingdom of God fulfill the Passover?
3. John's Gospel account does not mention the institution of the Lord's Supper. What are some of the other ways Passover themes are present in John's account?

FIRST MOVEMENT

• • • •

OUT OF
THE HOUSE
OF SLAVES

3

From the Bulrushes
to the Bush

Exodus 1–3

Long before Moses led the Israelites out of slavery in Egypt, he experienced two exoduses of his own. We often read these opening chapters so quickly, treating them as a glorified prologue to the blood-and-thunder, *Prince-of-Egypt* drama we know and love, that we miss this part of the story altogether (and this means we often miss the crucial role women play in the exodus story). But it's right there in the text. Moses has an exodus journey at birth, he has another at age forty, then he leads Israel in a third at age eighty, and then he dies at one hundred and twenty, right after seeing the land to which his whole life had been pointing. Quite a track record.

The first exodus comes in the midst of a plot that should be familiar to anyone who has read the garden story in Genesis. The people of Israel are fruitful and multiply and fill the land, but the serpent-like king is tricksy, and he attacks the women, with a view to destroying their male descendants. Yet in contrast to the garden story, the women outmaneuver him. First the midwives, then Moses's mother, and finally his older sister, Miriam, use their wisdom to beat the serpent at his own game, and preserve the seed of the woman. In fact, until Moses grows up, the only man who really features in the story is the dragon-like Pharaoh, hell-bent on destroying God's people.

It works like this. Moses's mother, Jochebed, knows there is something special about her baby boy, so she constructs an "ark," or basket, for him just as Noah had done (Exodus 2 is the only place in Scripture outside the flood story in which this word for "ark" appears). She covers it with pitch, just as Noah had done. While Pharaoh is building cities, an Israelite woman is building a tiny, unimpressive little ark for a child to be thrown into the water. Yet this ark, like Noah's, will become the vehicle through which God rescues the righteous from watery destruction, foils the plans of the wicked, and creates a new nation in the midst of the old.

Pharaoh's daughter hears the cry of the baby and takes pity on him, just as the Lord will hear the cry of Israel in slavery and take pity on them. Moses's basket is taken from amongst the reeds, just as Israel will be rescued through the Sea of Reeds. Moses is drawn out of the water even as others are drowned, just as Israel will later be, and it becomes a defining feature of his identity (the name "Mosheh" means "he draws out"), just as it will be for Israel. Miriam is the key witness to the event, just as she will be at the Red Sea. With his adoption by Pharaoh's daughter, Moses's exodus instantly transfers him from oppression into royalty, just as Israel's exodus will instantly turn them from oppressed slaves into royal priests. As Moses becomes part of an Egyptian family, we even get a hint of how Egyptians and Israelites will be joined together into one mixed multitude of covenant people, replete with Egyptian riches (Ex. 12:35–38). This is not the last time that Mosheh will be "drawn out."

Forty years pass. Israel's slavery continues. One day, Moses, stirred to action by the injustice of it, kills an Egyptian who is beating a fellow Israelite, and must flee from Pharaoh to the east and spend forty years in the wilderness. This part of the story is frequently used as an example of what not to do ("Moses tried to do God's work but ignored God's timing," or some such), but the narrator never suggests that application. In fact, the parallels with Moses's third and most dramatic exodus—in which Moses will be stirred to action, the suffering of the Hebrews will be noticed and then relieved, Egyptians will be killed, and Moses will flee Pharaoh to the east before spending forty years in the wilderness—suggest that Moses is foreshadowing Israel's later rescue, not bungling it.

His exodus takes him into the land of Midian, where his first recorded action is to fight off shepherds at a well and provide water for seven women and their flock. For all the sermons you hear on how David's time as a shepherd prepared him for national leadership ("your servant has struck down both lions and bears" [1 Sam. 17:36]), it is rare to hear one on the same pattern here, but notice: Moses will later defend the innocent against a false shepherd, using his own shepherd's staff, and then provide water in the wilderness for an entire nation. One of these women, Zipporah, becomes his wife, and he names their son Gershom (*gêr* means "sojourner"), saying, "I have been a sojourner in a foreign land" (Ex. 2:22). He speaks here not just for himself, but for the whole of Israel.

The climax of this second exodus story is the meeting with God on the mountain, in the burning bush. The similarities between this encounter and the subsequent encounter on Mount Sinai (which is also known as Mount Horeb) are remarkable: both involve an invitation to approach mingled with a warning not to come too close, both are accompanied by fire, both cause people to hide their faces, both are accompanied by miraculous signs, both summon Moses and Israel to respond in obedience, and both take place on the same mountain. But for all these similarities it is the revelation of the divine name, "I AM WHO I AM" (Exodus 3) or "The LORD, the LORD, a God merciful and gracious" (Ex. 34:6), that serves as the high point in each story. Key moments of rescue in Scripture are often accompanied by the revelation of God's name—God Almighty, God-Will-Provide, God-Is-My-Banner, the Rock, Immanuel, and so on—but these two revelations, both of which come toward the end of an exodus narrative, are the two to which the Scriptures most frequently return. Only by knowing God as the unchangeable, incomparable, eternal, self-existent, merciful, gracious, and compassionate God that he revealed himself to be on Mount Horeb can Moses, or Israel, or anyone who follows him today, have any hope of approaching, obeying, or worshiping him. "Whom shall I say has sent me?" we ask. "I AM," he says simply. So get on with it.

Finally, we come to one of the most puzzling stories in the whole Bible: the time when the Lord tried to kill Moses (Ex. 4:24–26). As odd as this story is when read out of context (which, owing to its strangeness, it often is), it is probably yet another example of what we have been seeing in this chapter, namely that Moses lives out the exodus story at least twice before he leads Israel out of Egypt. That is, we have in this short and rather painful story a foreshadowing, a musical prelude, of the Passover.

Look at it this way: It is night. Moses has just been told to warn Pharaoh that his firstborn son may be killed, because Israel is God's firstborn son. But Moses's own son has not been circumcised, which is the nonnegotiable mark of divine sonship for Israel. Moses has neglected God's commandment and now stands outside the mark of sonship, under the same judgment as Pharaoh. So, not for the first time, a woman comes to

Moses's rescue: Zipporah circumcises their son and puts the blood on display, "covering" Moses with it so that the Lord will not kill him. His son's foreskin becomes the Passover lamb, spread over the beams of his house at nighttime, and Moses is saved. You wonder whether one of the reasons Moses stressed obeying every detail of God's instructions on the first Passover (Exodus 12) was that, in this incident, he had seen something of what happens when you don't.

So Moses experiences an exodus at birth and another at age forty, complete with rescue by blood and through water (which may remind you of other places where salvation is accompanied by blood and water). By the time he reaches his third exodus, at age eighty, he might have a sense of déjà vu, or even be thinking, *Oh no, not again*. But God has fashioned Moses, quietly and secretly, into an exodus-shaped person. He has built toward the primary exodus with a series of smaller deliverances that gradually increased in intensity, like teaser trailers building toward the release of a movie. He has given the life of Moses and the life of Israel the same pattern, as Paul will later point out when he says that Israel was "baptized into Moses" (1 Cor. 10:2). God has demonstrated his sovereign control of history, building Moses's confidence for the future. Given the stakes, Moses will need every bit of faith in God's power to rescue, and every fragment of trust in the God who "draws out," that he can possibly lay hold of. So God's preparation, as lengthy and largely unnoticed as it is, is all vital groundwork. It always is.

Finally, with two exoduses already under his belt, Moses heads off to see Pharaoh. The stage is set for a showdown.

Review Questions

1. What are Moses's three exoduses? How did they form Moses into an "exodus-shaped" person?
2. How is Moses's deliverance as an infant similar to Israel's later deliverance at the Red Sea?

3. How does Moses's encounter with God when he was called at Mount Horeb resemble the later events at Sinai during the exodus?

Thought Questions

1. The birth of children is prominent in the opening two chapters of Exodus, and the theme of birth continues in the exodus story. Can you identify some of the hints in the text that suggest the exodus was like a birth for Israel itself?
2. Why might God have revealed his name to Moses at this particular time?
3. What might Israel have learned about itself from seeing the pattern of its deliverance in the life of its leader, Moses?

4

The Battle of the Gods

Exodus 4–15

The exodus is a battle of the gods, in which only one can emerge from the ring victorious. At the human level, all of the musical themes we are considering in this book—oppression, plagues, blood, redemption, escape, presence, water, victory, celebration, wilderness, inheritance—are here. But behind them all stands the conflict between the deities: Egypt's against Israel's, the false against the true, the serpent against the seed, Pharaoh against the Lord. It is a mismatch. Battles against the Lord always are.

We get a sense of this before the confrontation with Pharaoh even begins. Moses, you will remember, is worried that the Israelites will not believe him, so God gives him three signs, each of which point forward to the war to come (Ex. 4:1–9). First, God tells him to throw his staff onto the ground, and it becomes a serpent. Moses is scared, but when he takes hold of the serpent by the tail, it hardens back into a staff. Pharaoh, the serpent and destroyer, may be frightening, but when Moses takes hold of him by the tail, he will be hardened and ultimately turn into a rod by which God will fulfill his purposes ("I will harden Pharaoh's heart . . . and I will get glory over Pharaoh and all his host, and the Egyptians shall know that I am the LORD" [14:4]). Second, Moses puts his hand into his cloak, and it becomes diseased and unclean, and then he puts it back in his cloak again, and it emerges restored. God has the power to afflict and corrupt and also the power to restore and make alive, and the battle to come will see both at work. Third, God tells Moses that if he takes water from the Nile and pours it on the ground, it will turn to blood. One of Egypt's gods, and its primary source of livelihood and purity, will become a river of death, in a sinister echo of the attempt to drown Israel's boys. The battle lines are drawn.

Pharaoh, as predicted, refuses to let Israel go, and the war of the gods begins. The plagues, like many invasions, gradually escalate. They build in intensity: the early plagues affect everybody, and can be reproduced by Pharaoh's magicians, whereas the later ones affect only Egypt, and cannot be reproduced. But they also escalate in a literal and geographical sense. The first group of three plagues strikes the water and the ground, as the Nile bleeds, frogs rise up from the water, and the dust turns to gnats. The second group strikes living flesh, with swarms of flies, the death of livestock, and human skin being covered in boils. The third group moves higher, up to the skies, bringing destruction through the weather, bringing locusts on the east wind, and even blackening the sun. If the ancient world were a three-story house—the earth, the waters beneath, and the heavens above—God brought destruction to each story and humiliated the deities that "governed" each. The Egyptian gods were ferreted out and removed from the house, like a pest or an infestation, from cellar to rafter.

Finally, and climactically, Moses pronounces the tenth plague: the death of the firstborn son. We can try to soften the horror of this by pointing out important contextual factors—the repeated warnings, the way the deaths of Egyptian sons echo the deaths of Israelite sons earlier, the fact that firstborn sons represented the strength and future destiny of the ancient family, the oppression of Israel as *God's* firstborn son, the larger narrative in which Israelite freedom will lead to Egyptian salvation, the ongoing war between the seed of the serpent and the seed of the woman, and so on—but many of us will still find the story deeply troubling. This book does not attempt a defense of God's right to kill people, and Scripture doesn't either. But it is worth noting that, for all our questions and concerns, the narrative doesn't dwell on what happens to Egypt, giving it only two verses (Ex. 12:29–30). It is far more interested with the institution of the Passover.

Shelves could be filled with books on the significance of Passover, and probably have been. In a number of ways, the Passover is an obvious prelude to the work of Christ. It is about redemption from slavery by the blood of a lamb. It is about a sacrifice that passes through the fire and saves people from death, when everyone around them is facing judgment. It is about the power of faith worked out through obedience. Israelite families were not saved by their personal godliness that night or even by the amount of confidence they had in God They were saved simply by the fact that the blood was over their house.[1]

But the Passover also carries a number of less obviously "Christian" meanings. It is about purity: a spotless lamb, the removal of leaven, a seven-day festival, and hyssop dipped in blood are all required. It is about suffering: the bitter herbs remind future Israelites of the way things were before they entered a land flowing with milk and honey. It is about unity: entire households eat an entire lamb, with none of its bones broken and none left over until the morning. It is about the nature of memorial: much of the text focuses on the way Israel's life, liturgy, and worship will be shaped by the Passover celebration in the future. It is about the blessing of the nations: a "mixed multitude" is joined to Israel (12:38) and allowed to share Passover as long as they are circumcised. It is about childbirth: as Egypt becomes a tomb, covered in darkness and ash, Israel steps out from the womb through doorposts covered in blood, sets apart the firstborn sons, and later emerges into new life from a narrow passage through waters, which then close again behind them.

And so, in the middle of the night and without even a dog growling at them (Ex. 11:7), Israel begins the great escape. They are accompanied by untold numbers of Egyptians (representing God's global blessing), huge material wealth (his abundance), Joseph's bones (his faithfulness to his promises), and a pillar of cloud and a pillar of fire (his presence), as they flee the land of oppression. One more obstacle remains, however. Before Israel is to be truly free, they have to pass through the waters.

The boundary-marking power of water must be one of the hardest aspects of the exodus story for modern people to grasp, in our world of bridges and tunnels, ferries and airplanes. (Remarkably, there is not a single reference to bridges in the entire Bible.) In the biblical landscape, waters divide. The waters above are divided from the waters below, so if you want to descend to the depths or ascend to the heavens, you have to pass through water. The waters are divided from the dry land. The lands are divided by the great rivers, which makes a river crossing more like entering another country than driving across a bridge. Water even divides time as well as space, separating one era from the next: Noah passes through the flood into a new world; Jacob fords the Jabbok into a new name; Joshua crosses the Jordan into a new land; and John baptizes people into a new kingdom. Only when Jesus comes and pours out living water do we find the world's divisions finally disappearing—Jew and Greek, male and female, slave and free (Gal. 3:28)—in the waters of baptism.

As Moses raises his staff, and with the Egyptian army in pursuit, God divides the waters. This is true physically, in that dry land genuinely appears between two bodies of water, as it did on the third day of creation. But God also uses the waters to divide one nation from another, separating the Israelites from the Egyptians, with the former brought safely onto dry land and the latter brought down to the depths. As the cloud of God's presence comes between the armies (Ex. 14:19–20), it is as if the sky has come down and landed above Egypt and beneath Israel, taking Israel up into a new, heavenly space. Israel crosses at night but walks in the light of God's cloud into freedom; Egypt crosses as the day dawns but is thrown into a panic and covered by watery darkness. The night of slavery is over. Morning has broken.

And most importantly, the battle of the gods has been won. We might find it surprising, but this is what Israel sings about: not freedom, hope, or redemption, but the Lord's victory over Pharaoh, his armies, and his gods. Israel's God, riding his throne-chariot of cloud and fire, has crushed the dragon and hurled him into the depths. "The LORD is my strength and my song. . . . The LORD is a man of war; . . . Pharaoh's chariots and his host he cast into the sea. . . . Who is like you, O LORD, among the gods?" (Ex. 15:2–4, 11). Children's Bibles and Disney movies are filled with the miraculous drama of Israel's rescue, but the mouths of God's people are filled with the victory of God.

Not for the last time.

Review Questions

1. What patterns can we see in the ordering of the plagues?
2. How did the plagues function as a "battle of the gods"? What do they teach us about God?
3. Why are water crossings so significant?

Thought Questions

1. The introduction of the institution of the Passover in Exodus 12:1–2 removes us from the immediacy of the action of the preceding and following narrative and places us in the position

of looking back at the events from the perspective of those no longer in Egypt. What might this teach us about the relationship between the continuing celebration of the Passover and the original historical events?
2. Why does Moses use a rod?
3. How does the Song of the Sea in Exodus 15 look forward to the future of Israel?

5

True Freedom

Exodus–Deuteronomy

Escaping from Egypt is only the first half of the exodus. It is easy for us to forget this, in an age where freedom is understood as merely being freedom *from*: from oppression, from constraint, or whatever. This aspect of liberation, as wonderful as it is, is only half the deal. In the Scriptures, more emphasis is placed on the freedom *for*: for worship, for flourishing, for growth in obedience and joy and glory. Human beings are not designed to be free from all constraint, slaves to nothing but our own passions, triumphantly enthroned as our own masters, even our own gods. Everybody serves somebody. So the point of the exodus is not just for Israel to find deliverance from serving the old master. It is for them to find delight in serving the new one.

This powerful truth is at the heart of Christian discipleship. The opening question of the Heidelberg Catechism, one of the most beautiful statements of Christian doctrine, asks, "What is your only comfort in life and in death?" The answer is profound, exodus-shaped, and delightful: "*That I am not my own*, but belong, body and soul, in life and in death, to my faithful Savior Jesus Christ." The freest people in the world are those who are owned by someone else. Service is liberty. Obedience is joy.

That was God's endgame with the exodus all along. Back in the burning bush, he described Moses's mission like this: "When you have brought the people out of Egypt, you shall serve God on this mountain" (Ex. 3:12). You are currently servants to Pharaoh, God explained, but when we're done, you will be servants to me. As it turns out, freedom from serving Pharaoh is the easy bit. From beginning to end, it takes only fourteen chapters. Freedom to serve God, on the other hand, takes forty years of wandering and the next four books.

The second half of the exodus begins with Israel's journey to Sinai, which echoes the burning-bush journey of Moses in various ways. Israel, like Moses, finds food and water in the wilderness: the sweetening of the water, the arrival of manna and quail, and then water from the rock (Ex. 15:22–17:7). Israel, like Moses, fights off enemies at the source of water, triumphing through a shepherd's staff (17:8–16). Then, like Moses, Israel meets Jethro, who provides food and friendship (18:1–27), before arriving at Mount Sinai/Horeb, where the people are given both a commission and commandments (19–20). They also have two divine names revealed to them in the process (God-Heals-You and God-Is-My-Banner), just as Moses did (Yahweh and I AM THAT I AM).

The two halves of the exodus—freedom from serving Pharaoh and freedom to serve God—are summarized brilliantly at the start of the first commandment: "I am the LORD your God, who brought you out of the land of Egypt, out of the house of slavery. You shall have no other gods before me" (Ex. 20:2–3). The shape and nature of this service to the Lord is then filled out across the next nine commandments, and to this day, those ten rules encapsulate the shape of a life lived in liberated obedience. When the Ten Commandments are finished, to our surprise, the very next law concerns something quite obscure: what happens when a slave loves his master and wants to continue serving him even after he is entitled to leave (21:1–6). Yet a bit of reflection shows that even this reinforces the wider point about true freedom. When slaves, like Israel, love their masters, they will choose lifelong service over walking away. And the fact that the process for doing this involves blood and a doorpost (21:6) cannot help but remind us of the Passover.

Two major events dominate the rest of the book of Exodus, and both involve building a place of worship: the golden calf and the tabernacle, the false and the true, the problem and the solution. Israel's worship of the golden calf is a classic fall story, with a command broken by the priest left in charge (Adam/Aaron), the blame shifted to someone else (Eve/Israel), the exposure of shame, a curse involving eating (dust/powder), death, the establishment of sword-wielding guardians (cherubim/Levites), and the separation of God from his people. It is the low point of Israel's story so far. Yet Moses, the mediator, intercedes for Israel and urges God to continue dwelling among his people. The Lord relents, shows Moses his glory, reveals his name, and renews the covenant (Ex. 34:1–35), before coming to dwell in the tabernacle in glory as the book concludes (40:34). This key moment—"and Moses was not able to enter the tent of meeting because the cloud settled on it, and the glory of the LORD filled the tabernacle" (40:35)—marks a partial reversal of the fall, with a new Adam in a new garden and the dwelling place of God established again among humans. It also marks the undoing of Israel's slavery: instead of being forced to build Pharaoh's cities using bricks without straw, they have been invited to build God's house with the best of their gold and silver. Israel, despite their disobedience, has now well and truly left the household of Pharaoh and joined the household of God, their new master.

Leviticus, Numbers, and Deuteronomy all, in their own ways, elaborate on what the freedom to serve the Lord looks like in practice. Leviticus is mostly a book of regulation, set at Sinai, and focuses on fellowship with God. Numbers is mostly a book of rebellion, set on the wilderness journey, and focuses on faith in God. Deuteronomy is mostly a book of reiteration, set in the land across the Jordan, and focuses on following God, culminating in the glorious promise that one day God will circumcise Israel's hearts and not just their flesh. As hard as these books can be to read in places, their significance in the biblical story is massive, as they explain and show what the freedom to serve God—which was the whole point of the exodus in the first place—does and does not look like.

In Numbers, we also have something of a second exodus. Having been camped at Sinai for a year, Israel, including any foreigners among them, keeps the Passover (Num. 9:1–14), and then, led by the pillars of cloud and fire, moves out on their journey. They meet Jethro's son, and travel for three days (10:29–36). They complain to Moses, and Moses laments that he is not able to do the job on his own, with the result that his leadership load is spread among the elders (11:1–30). God, once again, provides quail from the sky (11:31–35), water from the rock (20:1–13), and military victory (21:21–35). All of these echo the first exodus.

As they did in the first exodus, however, Israel falls. Spies steal into the land of Canaan to prepare for an invasion, but they bring back a bad report. Moses was on God's mountain for forty days, and Israel builds a golden calf; the spies are in God's land for forty days, and Israel abandons their destiny (Num. 14:1–12). Once again, Moses intercedes for them. Once again, God agrees not to destroy them, although a plague strikes some of the witnesses. This is not the last of Israel's rebellions: the leadership attempts a coup (16:1–50), and, worse, the people engage in mass idolatry and sexual immorality at Moab (25:1–18), which resembles the golden calf incident so closely that we even have the same violent outcomes (a plague that brings death and a Levite taking up arms to kill idolatrous Israelites). This second exodus shows that God has not stopped loving Israel—but it also shows that Israel has not stopped loving evil.

The greatest threats to true freedom, it seems, do not come from external oppression but from within. Delivering Israel from slavery to Pharaoh took only ten plagues; delivering Israel from slavery to self, sin, sex, greed, and idolatry took ten commandments and ten separate trials and corresponding judgments (Num. 14:22), and ended up with an entire generation dying in the wilderness—and even then, the problems persisted. True slavery is captivity of the soul, not just the body. Until a nation or a person is freed from that, and free to become what they were originally intended to be, their exodus is incomplete.

Cultural critic Neil Postman makes a similar point by comparing the scenarios in Aldous Huxley's *Brave New World* and George Orwell's *1984*. Orwell, he explains, imagined a future in which our freedom is destroyed by external forces (spies, prisons, torture chambers, the state), whereas Huxley imagined one in which our freedom is destroyed by enemies within (innate desires, egotism, hedonism, leisure)—and Huxley, not Orwell, was right.[1] A contemporary parallel emerges in Suzanne Collins's *The Hunger Games*: the fatuous, green-haired, celebrity-obsessed crowds in the Capitol are in many ways more captive, less free, and more pitiable than the bread-starved vagrants in District 12. Their chains are invisible, but they are no less enslaved.

Biblical freedom involves both halves of the exodus journey. It means being rescued from both Orwell's and Huxley's nightmares, the tyranny of the other and the tyranny of the self, Egyptian enslaving and Israelite craving. Many people today, like citizens of the Capitol and of Huxley's *Brave New World*, do not see it that way; like the Judeans in John 8, they are likely to think they have no particular need of freedom, since they have never been enslaved to anyone. But for readers of the exodus story, the problem and solution are exactly what Jesus told those same Judeans. "Everyone who practices sin is a slave to sin. . . . So if the Son sets you free, you will be free indeed" (John 8:34, 36).

Review Questions

1. How might the exodus story challenge our culture's beliefs about freedom?
2. How does Israel's story follow the pattern of Moses's story?
3. In what ways does the story of the golden calf represent a fall story?

Thought Questions

1. How does the tabernacle relate to Mount Sinai?
2. How does the exodus theme of deliverance from slavery in order to enter into the service of a new Master illuminate the gospel message?
3. Why did the painful experiences of the wilderness have to intervene between the deliverance from Egypt and the entrance into the Promised Land?

6

Journey's End

Joshua 1–7

The exodus journey finally reaches its destination as Israel crosses the Jordan and enters the Promised Land. Until the conquest of Canaan, it feels like the exodus story is incomplete; we know that Israel is supposed to live in houses rather than camps, eat milk and honey rather than manna and quail, and ultimately worship at a temple rather than a tent. Yet the book of Joshua does not merely bring one story to completion. In keeping with the musical nature of Scripture, it concludes the exodus movement, while at the same time recapitulating it with all sorts of subtle variations, which themselves point forward to the melodies and rhythms that will shape the movements to come.

Even a small child, hearing the story for the first time, notices the similarities between the crossing of the Red Sea and the crossing of the Jordan. The two crossings are so similar that, in a number of places in Scripture, they are blurred together. "The sea looked and fled; Jordan turned back," says Psalm 114:3. In their song of triumph on the banks of the Red Sea, Israel had celebrated the inheritance of the Land as if it had already happened: "You brought them in and planted them on the mountain of your own possession" (Ex. 15:17 NRSV). Passages like these point to the fact that the journey out and the journey in are essentially one; the water crossings bookend the wilderness journey as an intermediate period that Israel was never intended to remain in. If waters in the ancient world were like national borders today, then we could compare the whole journey to catching a cross-channel ferry: we cross the UK border at Dover and the French one at Calais, but in between them we are at sea, neither in one country nor the other, waiting for the journey's end. So the similarities between Israel's two border crossings are highly significant, in that they help us see the exodus journey as fundamentally a whole—from Egypt to the Promised Land, from England to France—rather than a series of two or more separate incidents.

This sense of wholeness, and of completion, is borne out by all sorts of little connections between the journey out and the journey in. The period of wilderness wandering began with sending spies into Canaan, and it ends the same way (Joshua 2). Moses's life was saved as a baby through the trickery of a courageous woman, and the same is true for the Israelite spies saved by Rahab. Israel's first actions after crossing the Jordan are to set up a memorial, circumcise the men, and celebrate the Passover (Joshua 4–5), just as Israel did before crossing the Red Sea. The manna that God provided after the Red Sea crossing stops as soon as they eat the fruits of the land (Josh. 5:12). Joshua then meets the commander of the Lord's army and has to remove his sandals (Josh. 5:13–15), just as Moses had when he first encountered God. From there, Israel brings destruction on Jericho, yet spares those who have a crimson cord hanging from their window, just as the Lord's angel brought destruction on Egypt, yet spared those with crimson lamb's blood smeared across their doorpost.

Not only that, but the life of Joshua recapitulates the life of Moses. Both are chosen by God, have divine encounters at the start of their leadership, stretch out their hands for victory, unite the nation with the help of the elders and officials, receive confirmation of God's presence with them, send spies, deal with rebellious Israelites, build altars, mediate between Israel and God, have their old age announced and then specified (120 years for Moses, 110 for Joshua), make departing speeches that challenge Israel to obedience, and are identified as "the servant of the LORD" (Deut. 34:5; Josh. 24:29). These echoes are important—not only because they confirm that the two stories are parts of a divinely orchestrated whole, but also because they introduce a theme that will reappear in Scripture, particularly in the New Testament. Desert prophets, associated with water, make way for land prophets associated with rescue. Moses commissions Joshua ("The Lord Saves"). Elijah hands over to Elisha ("God Saves"). John the Baptist prepares the way for Jesus ("The Lord Saves"). You get the idea.

When you compare the Moses and Joshua stories, the most obvious twist is that the key events happen in reverse order. The journey in starts with spies, then a water crossing and memorial, then Passover and circumcision, then destruction; the journey out began with destruction, then Passover and circumcision, then water crossing and memorial, then spies. But the Joshua story has other twists and variations too, which do not merely echo or complete the original exodus, but subtly change it in ways that will become significant as Israel's story develops. The object that causes the waters to stop flowing is not the staff of a prophet, but the ark of the Lord. As Israel crosses the water, God's presence is not behind them, but ahead of them. The woman whose trickery saves Israelite lives is a Gentile prostitute, rather than an Israelite midwife or mother. Rahab's "Passover," in which a crimson symbol over her house saves her whole family from destruction, is given specifically to a Gentile woman, rather than Israelite men. Hope is stirring.

The musical echoes between the Red Sea and Jordan crossings can also, perhaps surprisingly, help us make sense of the violence in Joshua which we find so troubling. When we read the two stories alongside each other, and see the conquest of the land as the completion of the exodus, the parallels suggest two further significant points.

The first is that the instrument of God's judgment is now the people of Israel, rather than the angel of death. Israel is not, as it is often suggested, the primary agent in the story, invading a land that belongs to someone else, motivated by desire for territory, and then using divine sanction to justify it. Quite the opposite, actually: God is the primary agent of judgment, and he is using Israel as his instrument, much as he had previously used the angel on Passover night. The narrative makes this very clear. The walls of Jericho fall at the sound of the trumpets, not through Israel's military might (which becomes, literally, ridiculous as they march around the city). The commander of the Lord's army, when asked by Joshua whether he is "for us, or for our adversaries," famously answers "No." (Josh. 5:13–14). Furthermore, in contrast to the practice of "ethnic cleansing" or "genocide," faithful Canaanites (Rahab and family) are saved, and faithless Israelites (Achan and family) are destroyed. A great deal more could be (and has been) said about how we should read the conquest stories, but the parallel between the angel and Israel shows us that, whatever else we may say about them, Israel is the instrument for achieving God's purposes, not the other way around.[1] The battle is the Lord's, not theirs.

Second, we realize that the tragic story of Achan, who steals some of the devoted things from Jericho and keeps them for himself, is another fall story, equivalent to the building of the golden calf. We might even have seen it coming: Israel has been led through the water and given victory over their enemies, but instead of destroying the remnants of idolatry, they use them for themselves, with the result that three thousand people are defeated in battle, Joshua tears his clothes and cries out to God in despair, and God calls the people to execute judgment on those who have sinned (Josh. 7:1–26). (In the first exodus story, of course, the idolatry is committed by the entire nation, and three thousand people are killed, rather than merely fleeing in battle.) This reminds us, if we still needed reminding, that Israel's inheritance of the land does not mean they are now perfect, any more than their liberation from Egypt did. Fascinatingly, this fall pattern returns for a third time in the New Testament. No sooner has God's presence come to his people and begun to give them victory as a community than a household tries to steal from God and ends up killed (Acts 5:1–10). Ananias and Sapphira are the new Achan, and Peter the new Joshua.

Having said all that, the main thing we can see as Israel's exodus journey ends—at least for now—is God's faithful commitment to bring his people into freedom. We have seen unbelief and grumbling, rebellion and greed, insurrection and idolatry, but we have also seen a God whose covenant promises to his children will be kept, come what may. As Joshua leads his people into a land flowing with milk and honey, complete with cities they did not build and vineyards they did not plant, we are reminded that one day freedom will come, and a true and better Joshua will bring God's people through the waters, rescue prostitutes and sinners and Gentiles, and provide them all with an inheritance of peace, abundance, and rest. Just not yet.

Review Questions

1. In what ways does the entrance into the Promised Land recall the departure from Egypt?
2. How do the ministries of Moses and Joshua relate to each other?
3. What are the lessons of the story of Achan?

Thought Questions

1. How is the story of Rahab a Passover narrative?
2. How does Jesus fulfill the story of Joshua?
3. How might the musical character of the exodus in Scripture help us to understand the meaning of the Promised Land?

SECOND MOVEMENT

• • • •

THE EXODUS
IN GENESIS

7

People of Rest

Genesis 6–9

The story of humanity begins with an exile, not an exodus. That is the tragedy of the garden. Instead of leaving a place of slavery and heading for the land flowing with milk and honey, we begin our story by leaving the land of abundance and joining the world of thorns and thistles, labor pains and death. In a sense, the exile from Eden is like Israel's journey *into* Egypt, preparing us for the liberation of God's people, and ultimately his world, from oppression and frustration, which will ultimately be accomplished in Jesus. In the meantime, however, it also sets the stage for the numerous exodus stories that follow. The first of these comes to Noah.

The world of Genesis 3–6 looks strikingly similar to the world of Exodus 1–2. We have the righteous and the wicked, and the wicked are oppressing the righteous, even to the point of killing them. Cain has murdered Abel. Lamech has killed a man, and his practice of polygamy may suggest that other men are being killed or enslaved. Angelic beings have taken whichever human women they choose, and the wickedness of humanity is so great that his every intention is only evil, continually. The earth is filled with violence.

At the same time, God has heard the cry of the innocent. They call upon the name of the Lord (Gen. 4:26), walk with God (like Enoch in 5:22), and have found favor in the eyes of the Lord as blameless (like Noah in 6:8–9). God, we discover, has determined to judge the wicked and liberate the righteous. An exodus is coming.

It starts with the birth of a child, and particularly with his name: *Noah*, or "Rest." Exodus stories often begin with the naming of little boys—Moses, Samuel, John, Jesus—and in this case the promise is that the world will find "rest" through him. Yet Noah, like Moses, will achieve this rest by dividing the world. His message of righteousness and trust in God will lead to the condemnation of the violent, even as they save his family (Heb. 11:7; 2 Pet. 2:5).

God's means of rescue is, of course, the ark. Owing to children's Bibles and scientific worries, many of us probably don't think about Noah's ark that much, but it is rich with symbolic significance. It is a pitch-covered vessel designed to keep people safe through water, like that which will later save Moses. Its construction is described in detail, with its three decks representing the three layers of creation (waters, earth, heavens). It is then filled with animal life; a new creation is launched in the middle of the old one. There are two of every animal, but seven pairs of every clean animal, indicating that sacrifice is coming. Noah, it seems, is going to be a new priest in a new world.

Most obviously, from an exodus perspective, the ark is the way God keeps his people safe from the watery judgment that comes on the wicked. Just as Israel and Egypt both enter the Red Sea but only one emerges safe on the other side, so Noah's family and the rest of the known world enter the floodwaters, but only one makes it out alive. Just as Israel escaped judgment at Passover as they went inside their homes and closed the doors, so Noah leads his family inside the ark, "and the LORD shut him in" (Gen. 7:16). Just as Moses sent out messengers to spy out the land, so Noah sends out a raven and a dove to see if the floodwaters have subsided. Just as God remembered Israel and led them to a mountain where he gave them a new covenant, new laws, and ultimately rest, so God remembers Noah (8:1) and brings him safely to a mountain, where he receives a new covenant, new laws, and a place of rest. Noah is Moses. Ararat is Sinai.

The parallels cut both ways, however. By now, we know to expect that exodus stories are often followed by fall stories, and that is exactly what happens here. God commissions Noah's family to be fruitful and multiply and fill the earth, and reiterates that they share the divine image. Noah begins well by planting a vineyard, a symbol of fruitfulness, completion, and rest (as the Promised Land is later associated with luscious grapes and abundant wine). The next thing we know, the Land of Promise has once again become the site of temptation and fall. Commission, fruit, temptation, sin, nakedness, shame, clothing, a curse, a blessing, and finally death: the story of Genesis 9 is painfully familiar. Noah's exodus has brought judgment on the wicked and freedom for the oppressed, but humans are still fallen and sin is still here. A greater exodus is still needed.

It is no wonder that Peter sees this whole story as a picture of baptism (1 Pet. 3:18–22). On its own, the flooding of the known world might not look like a promising analogy for the beginning of the Christian life. But Peter sees baptism as one more example of a frequent musical theme in Scripture: that God's people are repeatedly "brought safely through water" (v. 20). God has a regular habit of using water to divide his people from the world around them, and protecting them from judgment, so it is only natural that the start of the Christian life would be marked off by a journey through water. "Baptism, which corresponds to this, now saves you," Peter writes in verse 21 (causing flutters of concern to all good Protestants, but that's another story). We, like Noah, have found favor in God's eyes, been placed within One who can save us from the coming judgment, been sealed inside by the hand of God, and then been brought through water into a land of covenant, promise, and fruitfulness. A Christian is a *Noah*. We are people of rest.

Review Questions

1. How is the ark like the creation in miniature?
2. List some of the exodus themes in the flood narrative.
3. How does the flood help us to understand the salvation Christ brings?

Thought Questions

1. How might the story of the flood in Genesis have informed the way its first hearers understood the story of the exodus?
2. How is Noah like Adam?
3. What natural properties of water suit it for the prominence that it has in many stories of salvation?

8

Russian Dolls

Genesis 10–15

Abram lives an exodus-shaped life, from beginning to end. So do most members of his family (as we will see in chap. 9). As the father of a people whose identity is fundamentally shaped by their exodus experience, this may not be surprising; we have already seen how God often prepares people in the early stages of their lives for what they will face later (something he still does today, incidentally). Nevertheless, the number of variations on the exodus theme are remarkable.

It all starts with a building project. Nimrod, a descendant of Noah's son Ham, has founded the city of Babel. The descendants of Shem have moved east and joined in the construction of a city and a tower, hoping to make a name for themselves (rather than God), and to protect themselves from being scattered across the earth (rather than filling the earth, as God had commissioned them). For both of these reasons, the Lord is preparing to destroy the city and scatter the men who have built it. So as Abraham's exodus is about to begin, we have Semites serving a blasphemous, Hamite imperial building project, and God preparing to bring judgment on the people and humiliate the gods they serve. All of these melodies will reappear in Exodus 1.

Terah, Abram, and their family come from Ur, which is near Babel, in what we now call Iraq. As we are introduced to them, we get a couple of clues that Ur is not only a place of idolatry but also a place of barrenness. Haran, Abram's brother, dies there. Sarai, his wife, is infertile. Terah is leading his family away from Ur and toward the land of Canaan. They make it only halfway, and settle instead in Haran (which is presumably named after Abram's dead brother), where Terah himself dies. Abram's family, which we later discover is large and prosperous, is being led from a land of barrenness into a Land of Promise, together with all their flocks and herds. This is an exodus journey in the making.

Like Israel's journey out of Egypt, Abram's exodus happens in two stages, with a lengthy stopover in the middle. The delay in Haran resembles the delay in the wilderness: the older generation dies out, others from outside of the family are added, and the new generation is given the crucial instruction to go in and inherit the Land. This instruction is one of the key turning points in the whole of Scripture: "Go from your country and your kindred and your father's house to the land I will show you. And I will make of you a great nation, and I will bless you and make your name great, so that you will be a blessing. I will bless those who bless you, and him who dishonors you I will curse, and in you all the families of the earth will be blessed" (Gen. 12:1–3). Abram, like Moses and Joshua, does not chart his own course, but has to trust that the Lord will lead him ("the land I will show you"). The men of Babel, like Pharaoh, were building cities and seeking a name for themselves; Abram, like Israel, has to trust that he will be given a great name by God.

Abram journeys throughout the land, together with his household, "all their possessions that they had gathered, and the people that they had acquired in Haran" (Gen. 12:5). This is a large group—if Abraham has 318 fighting men (14:14), then the entire community may have numbered two thousand—and would certainly have attracted attention. As they move from the north to Shechem in the center, then down to Bethel and Ai, and finally into the Negeb in the south, they are doing what Joshua will later do, and claiming the land for the Lord. Yet this is no military conquest. Abram lifts no weapons and fights no battles; instead, he builds an altar on a mountain, establishing true worship, and calls upon—or proclaims—the name of the Lord (12:8), probably calling the Canaanites to worship him too. In a sense, it is a spiritual conquest, similar to that which Jesus will later bring about as he walks the same earth and proclaims the same God.

No sooner is Abram's first exodus complete than his second begins (Gen. 12:10–20). Abram and Sarai, like their future descendants, leave the land of Canaan as a result of famine and head for Egypt. While there, the life of the male is threatened and the female risks being taken as a captive bride, and both are saved only through deception. The beautiful Israelite is taken into Pharaoh's house. Because Pharaoh does not let the bride leave, God afflicts him and his household with great plagues. Pharaoh blames Abram for making trouble, when it is actually Pharaoh who is at fault.[1] Eventually Pharaoh releases them: "take her, and go" (v. 12:19). As they leave, they take Pharaoh's slaves with them, along with all the possessions they have gained while in Egypt, and they arrive back in the land of Canaan far richer than when they had left it. (Notice that a number of these themes—the attack upon the bride, escape through deception, divine plagues upon the ruler, and the giving of spoils—reappear when Abraham and Sarah stay in Gerah in Genesis 20. Personal exoduses, it seems, are habit-forming.)

It is fascinating to watch. We see the exodus story played out in Abram's life, then in his extended family, then in the entire nation which comes from him, and then in the greater exodus accomplished in Jesus. It is like looking at a row of Russian dolls of increasing size lined up next to each other. Not only do the dolls look similar, but they also fit inside each other, revealing an internal unity. Abram is able to sum up the entire nation of Israel in himself, not least in his exodus journeys, just as Jesus will. That type of summing-up-in-himself, in fact, is at the heart of the gospel. Things that are true of our representative become, graciously and gloriously, true of us.

We find the most explicit reference to the exodus in Abram's story in Genesis 15, where God makes a covenant with him. After promising Abram offspring like the stars of the sky and counting his faith as righteousness, God speaks to him about the exodus that will come to his future family. He identifies himself as "the LORD who brought you out from Ur of the Chaldeans" (v. 7), just as he will later identify himself as "the LORD your God, who brought you out of the land of Egypt" (Ex. 20:2). He then specifies all the key details of the exodus story: Abram's seed will be in a foreign land; they will be enslaved and afflicted; their enslavement will last four hundred years; their oppressors will face judgment; and they will reenter the Land with great possessions. The ceremony that accompanies this covenant, which includes animal corpses cut in half, carries an intriguing resemblance to Passover. Great emphasis is placed on darkness, sacrificial animals, and a smoking fire pot and flaming torch of God's presence "passing through" the pieces. It is as if God is saying, not just in speech but in symbol: *Your family will be numerous, but they will face oppression. It will be long and painful. But you need to trust me. I am the God who brings out.*

As Abraham's seed, we still do. As Abraham's God, he still is.

Review Questions

1. How does the building of Babel foreshadow Israel's situation in Egypt?
2. List some of the ways in which the events of Genesis 12:10–20 resemble the later exodus.
3. What is the meaning of Abram's vision in chapter 15?

Thought Questions

1. What are some of the lessons that the Israelites might have learned about the character of God's activity in history from reading the story of Abram?
2. How might the narrative of Genesis 13–14 remind us of the conquest of the Land under Joshua?
3. What might the significance of the character of Melchizedek in Genesis 14:18–20 be in the context of this story?

9

Just Like Us

Genesis 16–26

Abraham is the fountainhead of God's people. As the Scriptures unfold, we find all sorts of ways in which his life is representative of his entire offspring—his call to bless all the nations, faith, credited righteousness, covenant, promises, and obedience. We hear echoes of his life throughout the pages of Genesis. So it is not surprising to find his exodus journeys reflected in the lives of his immediate family, including Hagar, Ishmael, Isaac, Rebekah, and Lot.

Hagar is the first woman in the Bible to experience an exodus all on her own, and she actually experiences two. In Genesis 16 an innocent slave (Hagar) is afflicted by her slave mistress (Sarai) and escapes into the wilderness of Shur, where she finds water in the desert, has an angelic encounter, receives promises of fruitfulness and blessing, receives revelation of God's name, sees God, and returns to the land of Canaan with divine blessing. The melody is then repeated in Genesis 21, but with an important variation. Hagar, like Moses, is alone in the first flight into the wilderness, but she takes the family with her in the second. She cries, and God hears the voice of her son (as he will when Israel cries) and provides for him (as he will for Israel), and the son lives in the wilderness of Paran (as Israel will). This is the exodus story in miniature.

Abraham's first two sons, Ishmael and Isaac, also experience exodus journeys, which harmonize closely with one another. Ishmael's begins when Abraham rises early in the morning, and the boy is taken by his mother into the wilderness. He nearly dies, but the angel of the Lord rescues him, as his mother opens her eyes and sees a well, and Ishmael receives God's promises and presence (21:9–21). Isaac's journey begins when Abraham rises early in the morning, and the boy is taken by his father into the wilderness. He nearly dies, but the angel of the Lord rescues him, as his father opens his eyes and sees a ram, and Isaac receives God's promises and presence (22:1–19). So, as in the exodus from Egypt, we have a journey into the wilderness, angelic rescue from the near death of the firstborn son, miraculous provision, and divine promises (on a mountain, in Isaac's case). For all the contrasts between Ishmael and Isaac that we find in Scripture, and there are many, we have a number of exodus-shaped similarities, too.

Then we have Isaac and Rebekah, whose exodus journey from Gerah in Genesis 26 is remarkably similar to that of Abraham and Sarah in Genesis 20. Famine drives them out of their own land and into a foreign country, where they deceive the king for their own protection (the wife/sister ploy again). They become extremely prosperous as a result of divine blessing. This growth makes them a threat to the local people, and the king urges them to leave: "Go away from us, for you are much mightier than we" (26:16). The Philistines have blocked all of Abraham's wells, which might remind us of the blocked wombs they experienced when Abimelech took Sarah into his harem (20:18). On leaving the land, Isaac and Rebekah move from place to place, struggling to find water in dry places and occasionally contending with their enemies, before eventually finding a place to settle. In light of the Joshua story, it is striking that Isaac names the place Rehoboth ("room"), saying, "For now the LORD has made room for us, and we shall be fruitful in the land" (26:22).

Most dramatic of all is the story of Lot and his family and their narrow escape from Sodom. The connection between Sodom and Egypt is first introduced in Genesis 13:10, with both described as "well watered everywhere like the garden of the LORD," and this natural fertility is why Lot chose to live in Sodom in the first place. But from the moment the Lord appears in Abraham's doorway in Genesis 18, we find a flurry of connections between the exodus from Sodom and the exodus from Egypt. God promises a son to Abraham and Sarah, announcing the end of their period of barrenness, and immediately goes on to judge the wicked city, accompanied by two witnesses (like Moses and Aaron). The rite of circumcision is instituted or established just beforehand. The angels are passing by (18:3–5), just as they will later in Egypt. An evening meal of unleavened bread is eaten (19:3). There is a threat to life at a doorway, and the angels haul Lot back inside and shut the door, to protect him from the judgment to come (19:4–11). God urges Lot to leave the city with all his relatives and possessions, because the "outcry" against the city has reached the Lord's ears (19:12–14). The angels lead Lot and his family out, and urge him to head for the mountain, lest he be "swept away" (19:15–17). As the sun rises, destruction from heaven falls upon Sodom and Gomorrah (19:23–25). Lot's family escapes the city alive, thanks to divine protection, and a pillar of witness is established (19:26).

At the same time, Lot's exodus is in many ways an anti-exodus, contrasting with the exoduses of Abraham that bookend it on both sides. Lot wants to go back to a place like Egypt, rather than to escape it, and as a result he loses possessions rather than gaining them. Lot's doorway, unlike the doorways in the Passover and Abraham stories, becomes a place of threat and death, rather than rescue and promise. Both Lot's sons-in-law and Sarah think that God's promise is a joke, but whereas the laughter in Abraham's family is followed by new life—and a child named *Isaac*, or "laughter"—the laughter in Lot's family leads to destruction. Abraham's wife is miraculously made fruitful; Lot's wife is miraculously made barren as a pillar of salt. Abraham lives in a tent and becomes the father of many nations by his wife. Lot lives in a cave, a symbol of the grave, and becomes the father of two nations by his incestuous daughters (19:30–38).

What do we make of all these exodus journeys amongst Abraham's family? At one level, they remind us that God is orchestrating history, Scripture, and the individual circumstances of his people, and has been since the beginning. At another, they show us the solidarity between Abraham and the members of his family—what happens to him happens, somehow, to them—which is itself an important ingredient in the gospel, as Paul will explain with such passion in Romans and Galatians. But there is at least one musical phrase in the story of Abraham's family that appears nowhere else, and it is enormously encouraging for the Christian life. Lot, like all of us, is rescued *in spite of himself*.

The other exodus stories we have seen so far involve a cry for help, or at least some awareness on the part of the oppressed that there is a problem. Here, by contrast, the cry that reaches heaven is an outcry against the city, not a cry for help from within it. Lot is ensconced in Sodom, oblivious to the judgment heading his way. He is not particularly looking to be rescued. He is an elder in the city (19:1), and even as destruction is coming, he lingers (19:16). He is staring death in the face, and he doesn't even know it.

Yet God, in his grace, saves him anyway. Lot does not particularly care about being saved, but the priestly prayers of his righteous family member avail for him—"Shall not the Judge of all the earth do what is just?"—even though Lot doesn't know anything about them (18:25). At Abraham's request, God intervenes. Angels visit Lot's house, compel him back indoors when danger comes, and urge him to flee along with his family. When, in spite of all of this, he still stays put, "the men seized him and his wife and his two daughters by the hand, the LORD being merciful to him, and they brought him out and set him outside the city" (19:16). He is dragged away from fiery destruction by the hand of God, not because of anything he himself has done, but because of God's mercy.

Just as we are.

Review Questions

1. How do Isaac's and Ishmael's stories resemble each other?
2. How is Lot's deliverance from Sodom exodus-shaped? How does it invert exodus themes?
3. How are Lot and his wife contrasted with Abraham and Sarah?

Thought Questions

1. Identify some of the fall themes in the story of Hagar's expulsion in Genesis 16.
2. The stories of Genesis 12:10–20, 20:1–18, and 26:1–11 are remarkably similar in several respects. What are some of the differences between them, and why might these be important for understanding their meaning?
3. The New Testament speaks on a number of occasions of Abraham as our "father." How do the repeated exodus themes of Genesis help us to understand what this means?

10

Wrestling with God

Genesis 27–50

It can be hard to tell the difference between an exodus and an exile, especially when you're in the middle of one. When Isaac's son Jacob first ran away from his brother, Esau, after tricking him out of both his birthright and his blessing, it must have felt like an exile: an extended period of servitude in a foreign land, despite possessing promises of fruitfulness and blessing. In truth, this was the opening scene of an exodus story, which culminated in the founding of a nation. But Jacob could not have known that.

Rebekah, Jacob's mother, had urged him to flee to her brother Laban's house in Haran, which is the very town where Abram had stayed on his journey from Ur to Canaan. The exodus setup is familiar by now. A member of Abraham's family heads to a new land, where he is at first welcomed, but gradually becomes diminished in status (treated as a servant rather than a relative), mistreated (tricked into marrying two daughters rather than one), and oppressed by a serpent figure (Laban). The women in the story are also mistreated by the serpent figure, who in this case is their father: Rachel is denied exclusive rights to her husband, and Leah is forced into marriage as an unloved wife. God, however, hears the cry of the oppressed women, and begins to bless them with children, who eventually lead the twelve tribes of Israel. Despite their oppression, Jacob's family prospers, is fruitful, and multiplies, and the opening scene concludes with the birth of the miraculous child, Joseph, who will later deliver them from disaster (Gen. 29:1–30:24). All of these themes will resurface in Exodus 1–2.

The birth of Joseph, like the birth of Moses, is the sign that the long period of servitude is about to come to an end: "As soon as Rachel had borne Joseph, Jacob said to Laban, 'Send me away, that I may go to my own home and country'" (30:25). Jacob, like Moses, approaches his master and asks to be allowed to leave, accompanied by his entire family. Laban, like Pharaoh, says no. After some negotiation, in which Laban shows himself once again to be a manipulative taskmaster, Jacob is allowed some independence with "a distance of three days' journey" (v. 36) between them, just as Moses will later demand from Pharaoh. Jacob, like Israel, plunders his former master—it is important to the story that his wages are *taken* rather than given—and grows enormously wealthy (vv. 25–43). He then receives an angelic commission to return to his homeland, flees from Laban with all he has, crosses a large river (the Euphrates), and heads for the mountain (of Gilead), until the third day (31:1–21). You couldn't make this stuff up.

Laban, like Pharaoh, is angry at being tricked, and gives chase. Yet instead of the showdown we might expect—Laban being swept away by a wall of water, or at least being afflicted with a few boils or something—we have the rather farcical anticlimax of Laban searching for his stolen household gods, all while his daughter Rachel is sitting on them, refusing to get up because it's her time of the month (31:25–35). Even this, however, reflects the exodus themes of women tricking the tyrant, and more importantly, the humiliation of false gods and their contrast with the real one. The God of Jacob's father has appeared to him at Bethel, accompanied him throughout his journeys, and brought him great prosperity. The gods of Leah and Rachel's father cannot even rescue themselves from being captured and then sat upon by a menstruating woman.

In a strange twist, Laban and Jacob then establish a covenant together. Although Laban's main role in Jacob's exodus story is to play the part of Pharaoh, in a curious sense he also plays the part of Jethro, the father-in-law who meets Israel just after their escape and establishes friendship. They mark the covenant by means of a heap of stones, just as Israel does before taking Jericho. Jacob's exodus journey is nearly over.

But not quite. First he has to undertake a nighttime crossing of the Jabbok, a tributary of the River Jordan, and to wrestle with an unnamed man until dawn (Gen. 32:22–32). The second river crossing has an obvious exodus connection: if the Euphrates (like the Red Sea) represents departure from servitude, the Jabbok (like the Jordan) represents entrance into inheritance, and we can see this worked out in Jacob's reconciliation with Esau and his safe arrival in the land of Canaan (33:1–20). The wrestling at Peniel is more subtle, though. It is as if Jacob has spent his life wrestling with men—Isaac, Esau, Laban—only to discover that he has actually been wrestling with God, in and through these individuals. It is very possible that, fording a river in the dark, Jacob thought that the man he was wrestling actually *was* Esau (whom he was scared of meeting) or even Laban (from whom he had been fleeing), which might explain his desperation to find out the man's name. Only as dawn is about to break does Jacob realize that he has been wrestling with God himself, and he receives a new name: *Israel*, or "he struggles with God" (32:28).

I wonder whether it was this scene that gave C. S. Lewis the idea of Shasta's conversation with Aslan in *The Horse and His Boy*. The young boy has been harassed by various lions throughout his journey, but as the story nears its climax, Shasta discovers that it was Aslan all along:

> I was the lion who forced you to join with Aravis. I was the cat who comforted you among the houses of the dead. I was the lion who drove the jackals from you while you slept. I was the lion who gave the Horses the new strength of fear for the last mile so that you should reach King Lune in time. And I was the lion you do not remember who pushed the boat in which you lay, a child near death, so that it came to shore where a man sat, wakeful at midnight, to receive you.[1]

Jacob, now named Israel, is in awe. "I have seen God face to face," he exclaims, "and yet my life has been delivered" (Gen. 32:30). This, of course, will also be the story of the nation to whom he gives his name.

Before Genesis closes we hear about one more exodus, which sets the scene for the great exodus to come under Moses: that of Jacob's favored son, Joseph (Genesis 37–45). Like Moses, Joseph is set apart from his brothers at birth and finds himself rejected by them, leading him into a wilderness in which he encounters violent shepherds and then has to wait a long time before bringing the deliverance he has been promised. Like Moses, Joseph brings rescue to an entire nation from the plague (in this case famine) that God is bringing upon Egypt, so that other nations might be blessed. Like Moses, Joseph is a prince of Egypt who ends up humiliating their gods as powerless before the Lord. Like Moses, Joseph leads his family/nation out of impending disaster into a land of abundance, but has to lead them first through a series of trials. Like Moses, Joseph dies in a manner that points forward to the inheritance of the Promised Land.

Yet unlike Moses, this is an exodus not out of Egypt, but into it. And in a manner only somewhat like Moses—but very much like Jesus—this is an exodus that Joseph experiences personally first. He is sold as a slave, wrongfully accused, thrown into the pit, raised up again, and exalted to the right hand of the Power. Only then, in and through him, do God's glorious blessings come to the world, and to his brothers. Hallelujah.

Review Questions

1. How is Jacob's sojourn with Laban like Israel's time in Egypt?
2. How does the wrestling with the angel shed light upon the broader character of Jacob's life story?
3. How is Joseph like Moses?

Thought Questions

1. How does the story of Genesis 25:20–34 remind us of the story of the fall?
2. We have already encountered several important stories of deception in the context of exodus-shaped stories. Can you list them? Can you think of further examples?
3. Can you think of any ways in which Jacob's struggle with the angel prefigures Christ's death?

THIRD MOVEMENT

• • • •

THE REECHOING
OF EXODUS

11

Wings of Refuge

Ruth

The book of Ruth is such a touching love story and such a charming tale of emptiness to abundance that we can easily think there is nothing more to it. Naomi loses her husband, her sons, and her joy, but one of her daughters-in-law sticks with her, gets married, and gives her a grandson. Boaz is one of the good guys and does the right thing even though he risks losing the woman he loves—but he wins her anyway. Ruth is bereaved and bereft, but then meets a man who is kind to her and who ends up redeeming and marrying her. They all live happily ever after.

There is, however, more going on here. From a historical point of view, Ruth is a crucial hinge in the story of Israel, marking the transition from the age of the judges to the age of the kings (which the writer highlights by starting the book with "in the days when the judges ruled," and finishing it with the word

"David.").[1] From a Christian point of view, the first two explicit Old Testament references to King David are in this book, and the way in which Ruth, as a Gentile woman, gets incorporated into Israel—through the kindness and redemption of a man from the tribe of Judah—has encouraged the church for centuries. And from a musical point of view, it is another exodus story. It is also, in many ways, an upside-down one.

Naomi is Israel. Famine is in the land, so she and her husband leave for a foreign country, where they are initially able to find food. But the place of plenty becomes a place of death to her: first her husband, Elimelech, then her sons, Mahlon and Chilion, die in Moab. While there, she hears that her homeland is now a place of abundance, so she leaves the foreign country to return home, taking her two (foreign) daughters-in-law with her. On the journey, the older one turns back, while the younger one continues toward the land, and they finally arrive in Bethlehem, the "house of bread." This story has a clear exodus shape.

Yet it is an exodus gone wrong, an exodus with a bitter twist. When Israel went down to Egypt to avoid famine, they multiplied and became numerous, and food and drink were supernaturally provided as they approached the land flowing with milk and honey. When Abraham, Isaac, and Jacob went abroad, they became wealthy, and returned home with prosperity and abundance. Exodus stories are supposed to involve people going out empty and coming back full.

But Naomi's exodus is not like this. "I went away full, and the LORD has brought me back empty," she laments (Ruth 1:21). She has lost her husband and her sons. She is unable to have more children. She is in need of food and land. She is so desperate that she gives herself a new name: "Do not call me Naomi; call me Mara, for the Almighty has dealt very bitterly with me" (v. 20). We hear darker notes than we are used to in exodus stories. The melody of redemption has been soured.

In many ways, Naomi's confusion reflects the state of Israel in the period of the judges. We have had our exodus, Israel might think, and we are now back in the land—but we are not living in the abundance we had hoped for. We are widowed. We face death every day. Our food, our children, our land, and our dignity are being taken by our enemies (think of Gideon in the winepress, for instance). The Lord has dealt bitterly with us. The God of the exodus has gone quiet. Where is his mighty hand or his outstretched arm? How long, O Lord?

When redemption eventually comes, it comes in a way that reveals all sorts of other exodus connections. Naomi is redeemed as she incorporates a foreign nation (in the form of Ruth) into her family, just as Israel was. Boaz, the redeemer, insists that the poor and the sojourner should be able to glean freely from the grain fields and invites Ruth to eat and drink at his table, just as the Lord did. Ruth ends up with far more food than she could possibly have gained for herself, thanks to the generosity of her redeemer, just as Israel did. Boaz redeems Ruth in order that he might marry her, just as God did with Israel.

One of the subtler echoes of the exodus is the language of "wings." As Israel arrives at Sinai having just been led out of Egypt, God describes their rescue like this: "You yourselves have seen what I did to the Egyptians, and how I bore you on eagles' wings and brought you to myself" (Ex. 19:4). As if to symbolize this, the cherubim that guard the ark of the covenant are built with outstretched wings, and the Song of Moses pictures God leading Israel like an eagle leads its young, "spreading out its wings, catching them, bearing them on its pinions" (Deut. 32:11).

God's wings disappear in Joshua and Judges, only to reappear again here, as Boaz describes Ruth's quest for safety in God: "[May] a full reward be given you by the LORD, the God of Israel, under whose wings you have come to take refuge" (Ruth 2:12). The God whose wingspan provides protection until the raging storm has passed by is present to bless Ruth and deliver her, as he was with Israel as they left Egypt. Ruth gets the point, and in that famous scene when she asks Boaz to redeem her, she urges him, "Spread your wings over your servant, for you are a redeemer" (3:9). Israel could have said exactly the same thing as they fled Pharaoh. The God of the exodus is back.

As the book reaches its conclusion, and the redemption of Ruth and Naomi is accomplished, we finally see how the musical themes in Ruth parallel not just the Lord's redemption of Israel from Egypt, but Christ's redemption of his people from sin. Like Ruth when she first meets Boaz, we are outsiders when we first meet Jesus: homeless, estranged, hungry, and empty. We come to him because we've heard that he is worthy, a man who blesses those in search of food and lifts the needy from the ash heap (1 Sam. 2:8). He says to us, as Boaz essentially says to Ruth, "Don't go anywhere else. Keep close to me, and I'll make sure you're looked after."

We look shocked, like Ruth, and ask: "Why have I found favor in your eyes, that you should take notice of me, since I am a foreigner?" (Ruth 2:10). Christ says to us: "The Lord repay you for what you have done, and a full reward be given you by the Lord, the God of Israel, under whose wings you have come to take refuge!" (2:12). He invites us to his table: Here, take bread, and dip it in the wine. We accept and lie down at his feet, asking for his wings of safety to cover us. He rescues us with joy and commits not just to redeem but also to "marry" us. And when those around us see the results of the gospel in our lives, they say what the women say to Naomi: "Blessed be the Lord, who has not left you this day without a redeemer!" (4:14).

Because of the God of the exodus, they all live happily ever after. For all the anguish of loss and displacement and waiting, Naomi ends the story no longer empty but full: "A son has been born to Naomi" (Ruth 4:17). So does Ruth, her outsider, widowed, Gentile daughter-in-law. So does Boaz, the worthy man who becomes the great-grandfather of David.

So do we.

Review Questions

1. How does the story of Ruth serve as a hinge in Israel's story?
2. Why might Naomi's experience be described as an exodus gone wrong?
3. How does Naomi's surprising redemption take an exodus shape?

Thought Questions

1. In what respects could Ruth be compared to the church?
2. What significance might there be to the fact that the events of Ruth 3 occur on a threshing floor?
3. How might registering the fact that Ruth is a Moabitess enrich our reading of key scenes in the book?

12

The Capture of God

1 Samuel 1–7

Scripture gives us many clues when an exodus story is about to begin. Evil rulers, for instance. Famines. Journeys into foreign lands. Women outmaneuvering powerful men. Battles between gods. The oppression of the innocent. A barren woman crying out for a child is a strong hint that a work of redemption is on its way. But if she then gets pregnant and bursts into song about how God is going to bring down the mighty and exalt the humble, it's a dead giveaway. Welcome to the world of 1 Samuel.

The prayers and courage of faithful women, and childless women in particular, are often the means by which God rescues his people from the tyranny and abuse of faithless men. Sarah, Rebekah, Rachel, the Israelite midwives, Ruth, Hannah, Abigail, Esther, Elizabeth, Mary: God revels in overthrowing strong through vessels of weakness. At the start of 1 Samuel it is Hophni and Phinehas, the sons of Eli the priest, who are abusing their privilege and oppressing the innocent, and it is Hannah, the childless wife, who is crying out in desperate prayer. And God hears. As with Israel in Egypt, the cry of Hannah goes up to the Lord, he "remembers" her (1:19), and when she has given birth to Samuel ("God hears"), she sings a song celebrating the way God is turning the world upside down (2:1–10). The mighty will be crushed. The feeble will be strong. The poor will be rich. A thousand years later, a pregnant young woman will pray almost identical things, with even greater significance (Luke 1:46–55).

Yet the rescue does not take the form we might expect. Reading 1 Samuel after reading all these exodus stories is like listening to a piece of music where a set melody has been established, and then suddenly hearing a totally unpredictable chord that confounds our expectations. When Hannah's little boy grows up, he does not lead Israel into a foreign nation and then out again. In fact, despite all our assumptions, it is God himself who goes into the foreign nation, and God himself who comes out again in triumph, having crushed his enemies. The tune is the same shape, but the key has changed.

Israel is at war with the Philistines. To compensate for an early defeat at Aphek, the elders of Israel decide to bring the ark of the covenant up from Shiloh, "that it may come among us and save us from the power of our enemies" (1 Sam. 4:3). The Philistine response—which, interestingly, appeals to the exodus from Egypt as motivation (4:8–9)—is to fight all the harder, and for the first and only time in history, the ark of God is captured by a foreign power. When he hears the news, Eli collapses and dies. Hophni and Phinehas fall in battle. The wife of Phinehas gives birth to a child she names Ichabod ("the glory has gone!"), and then dies. Not for the last time in 1 Samuel, the entire ruling dynasty has been laid waste in a single day.

The ark of the Lord, meanwhile, is taken captive. It is a mark of God's grace that he, substituting for the nation as a whole, goes into exile. Israel remains in the Land, while God takes on the consequences of their failures (again, not for the last time). But the Philistines get more than they had bargained for. As Pharaoh and Abimelech found with Abram and Sarai, and Egypt found with Israel, hosting the people of God is a dangerous game, particularly when you are trying to take advantage of them—and it is far worse when you try it with the presence of God himself. The morning after the Philistines put the ark in the temple of their god, they find Dagon bowing down before the Lord. Assuming some sort of unfortunate deity mishap—a slippery floor, perhaps?—they take Dagon "and put him back in his place" (1 Sam. 5:3). The scene the next morning is not pretty. Dagon has lost his hands and his head, like every defeated serpent. The battle of the gods has been won by the one true God.

Then the plagues begin. First the city of Ashdod, then Gath and Ekron, are struck with tumors as the ark is passed from town to town like a (very dangerous) hot potato. For anyone familiar with the disasters that struck Egypt, it is all too familiar: "The hand of the Lord was heavy against the people"; "The cry of the city went up to heaven" (1 Sam. 5:6, 12). The people urged their leaders to "send away the ark of the God of Israel" (5:11). Finally, the leaders "called for the priests and the diviners" to find out what to do (6:2), and they were given an emphatic answer: "Why should you harden your hearts as the Egyptians and Pharaoh hardened their hearts? After he had dealt severely with them, did they not send the people away, and they departed?" (6:6). Learning from Egypt's example, and their experience of being plundered by Israel at night, they decide to send the ark back to Israel complete with gifts—although, in a tragic but not unprecedented twist, God's "exodus" journey is marred by rebellion among the people (6:19–21), and the ark does not reach its final destination for another hundred years or so (2 Sam. 6:1–19).

Nevertheless, the story concludes where exodus stories usually do: with the successful conquest of the Land and the driving out of God's enemies. Samuel, like Joshua, gathers the nation and calls the people to put away their false gods and serve the Lord only (1 Sam. 7:3). After repenting and praying, Israel prepares for battle against the Philistines, only to find—as they did at Jericho—that the battle is won by God, through very unconventional means (7:10). Samuel even leads the people to set up a memorial stone, as Joshua had done after crossing the Jordan, and he names it Ebenezer ("stone of help"): "Till now, the LORD has helped us" (7:12). The tragedy of the Battle of Aphek has been reversed, and the Land is secure. The weak have been made strong and the powerful have been crushed, just as Hannah prophesied they would.

What Hannah never predicted, however, was the *means* by which this great reversal would take place. The story does not turn on the battlefield, through strategy or strength, at Aphek or Ebenezer. The story turns as the ark of the covenant is captured, placed before a foreign god in a foreign temple, and left there as a sign of God's defeat and humiliation. Like Samson a few years later, the ark is placed in the temple of Dagon to show Philistine strength and Israelite weakness, with all God's enemies mocking and gloating. And it is in this context—at the climax of the Philistines' victory—that the great reversal takes place. Israel's God triumphs, not *in spite of* his humiliation, but somehow *through* it. Samson, Israel's champion, bows his head, stretches out his arms, and kills more in his death than he had killed in his life. The ark of God saves a nation by being captured. And the head of Dagon is crushed.

One day, not far from the city of Ashdod, God will be captured again. He will be seized, paraded in front of foreigners and their gods, ridiculed, mocked, and humiliated. At the moment of his greatest weakness—naked, nailed, and bleeding, as his enemies spit and cast lots for his clothes—the great reversal will take place, and Israel's God will triumph not in spite of his humiliation, but somehow through it. Jesus, Israel's true champion, will bow his head, stretch out his arms, and save more in his death than he had saved in his life. The Son of God will save a nation by being captured. And the head of the dragon will be crushed.

Review Questions
1. Why might the story of Samuel begin with Hannah?
2. How does the capture of the ark lead to another battle of the gods?
3. How do the Philistines learn from the example of the Egyptians?

Thought Questions
1. How does Hannah's story and prayer illuminate the connections between her personal plight and that of the nation?
2. What are some of the similarities between the story of 1 Samuel 1–2 and the opening chapters of Luke and Acts?
3. How do the stories of the capture of the ark and the death of Samson help us to understand the manner of God's salvation displayed in Christ?

13

All about the House

1 Samuel 15–2 Samuel 24

Here's a thought experiment. Let's say we didn't know who had written any of David's psalms. Then let's say that we were told they were all written by the same major biblical character, and we had to guess which one. Who would we think had written them?

Think about it for a moment. The psalmist describes being pursued by enemies (Ps. 7:1) and sinking into the mire as the waters come up to his neck (69:1–2). He speaks of a change of fortunes in the early morning (143:8), being rescued from the rush of mighty waters (32:6), and seeing his enemies falling into the trap that they had set (9:15), while he is brought out of the bog onto solid ground (40:2). He talks about God being present in the clouds (18:11), and the angel of the Lord camping around him (34:7). He praises God for sending hailstones on his enemies, thundering from heaven, and exposing the channels of the sea by the blast of his nostrils (18:12–15). He rejoices at the defeat of those who trust in horses and chariots (20:7–8), and worships God the rock (18:2), for whom he longs as if desperate for water in the middle of a desert (63:1). He calls upon God to arise and let his enemies scatter (68:1). He celebrates the gift of the law (19:7–13) and the way God leads his people into a home of prosperity (68:6). If it weren't for all those references to "the king," I think we might guess that these psalms were written not by David but by *Moses*.

You could argue that this is nothing more than poetic imagery. The exodus story looms large in Israel's thinking, as we have seen throughout this book, so of course leaders would structure their songs around that story. But when we take a closer look at David's life, as it is told in Samuel and Chronicles, we see that David sang exodus-shaped songs because, from start to finish, he lived an exodus-shaped life.

Almost as soon as he is introduced, David is thrust into a high-profile confrontation with a powerful man whose nation is oppressing God's people. David against Goliath, like Moses versus Pharaoh, is a battle of the gods played out through two men, complete with the usual warnings, threats, and trash talk. The stakes are incredibly high: slavery for the loser, victory and land for the winner. As Pharaoh is described as a dragon who ends up getting pierced (Isa. 51:9; Ezek. 29:3), so Goliath is pictured as a villainous snake, covered in scaly armor (1 Sam. 17:5), lying in wait in the Valley of Elah and spewing forth accusations. David, like Moses, has no qualifications other than the experience of having kept sheep, and the fear of the living God. You know the result. Like the original serpent, and like the dragon in the depths of the Red Sea, Goliath ends up getting crushed, with his head bruised and eventually removed. Israel's men—despite their obvious fear of giants—rush up out of the valley in triumph, and the women pick up their tambourines and sing in victorious celebration. Israel's God is vindicated.

Yet the story is only just starting, because Goliath is not the only Pharaoh-like character David will face. No sooner has the spear-wielding Philistine been killed than we find, ominously, another character picking up a spear and using it to threaten the future king: "Saul had his spear in his hand. And Saul hurled the spear, for he thought, 'I will pin David to the wall'" (1 Sam. 18:10–11). The transfer of the spear shows us that the mantle of oppression has passed from Goliath to Saul, and with it, the threat to Israel's safety and inheritance. Saul is the new Pharaoh.

Like Pharaoh, Saul tries to kill the anointed leader while he is still young, but fails, ironically through the intervention of his own daughter. Like Pharaoh, Saul brings his adversary into his household. Like Pharaoh, Saul's attempts to destroy his rival lead to an escape at nighttime, through the substitution of an animal (1 Sam. 19:11–17). Like Pharaoh, Saul hardens his heart and pursues his opponent, to the eventual destruction of both himself and his family.

David, meanwhile, flees the pursuing king and ends up wandering in the wilderness. At the first place he stops he receives holy bread, the bread of the Presence, which reminds us of the manna provided from heaven for Israel (1 Sam. 21:1–6). He leads a grumbling group of malcontents in the middle of nowhere (22:1–5). He is opposed by Edomites, just as Israel was in the wilderness (22:11–19). He spends time in a foreign nation under a foreign king, is given a portion of land for himself, eventually leaves with a large company of people, and defeats the Amalekites (27:1–30:31). The striking difference is that whereas Moses and Israel sang for joy at the defeat of the king who was trying to kill them ("The LORD is a man of war!" Ex. 15:3), David sings a lament ("How the mighty have fallen!" 2 Sam. 1:19, 25, 27). Both the stories of Moses and David, contain two major songs: one in the middle, immediately after their enemy has been defeated (Exodus 15; 2 Samuel 1), and one at the very end, celebrating the faithfulness of the rock-like God who has led them to safety (Deuteronomy 32; 2 Samuel 22).

David's life is not all desert. Like Israel, he eventually leaves his wilderness wanderings and takes hold of the land God has given him. Echoes of Joshua's conquest are all over 2 Samuel: in the capture of the apparently impregnable fortress of Jerusalem (like Jericho), the kindness and inclusion shown to the would-be-enemy Mephibosheth (like Rahab), the hiding of the spies by a woman (2 Samuel 17), and the crossing of the Jordan to take the city (chap. 19). More tragically, like Achan in Joshua 7, first David (with Bathsheba) and then two of his sons (Amnon with Tamar, and Absalom with the kingdom) seize things which are forbidden, with catastrophic consequences for their families and the nation. And worryingly, the story ends with *David* as the Pharaoh-like king who wants to use God's chosen people for his own ends, and *Israel* as the ones afflicted by a plague by the angel of the Lord (2 Samuel 24). The land has been conquered, but it is not yet at rest. We are still awaiting a true Joshua.

Perhaps the most significant echo of the exodus story in David's life, however, has nothing to do with battles or plagues, enemies or deserts. When we stand back from the excitement of the individual incidents and consider the overall sweep of the story, David, like Moses, is the prophetic leader who hosts God's presence, draws Israel toward true worship, receives a covenant, and prepares a house for the Lord to dwell in. David brings the ark to Jerusalem. He desires to build God a house. He receives the covenant promise: "I will raise up your off-spring after you, who shall come from your body, and I will establish his kingdom. He shall build a house for my name, and I will establish the throne of his kingdom forever. I will be to him a father, and he shall be to me a son" (2 Sam. 7:12–14). He gets everything ready for the house of God, from musicians to money. That, in many ways, is his legacy. It is also the way in which he is most like Moses.

The book of Exodus, for most of us, has an exciting half and a boring half: the blood and thunder and escape (Exodus 1–19), followed by the law and the preparation of the tabernacle (20–40). The story of David, likewise, comprises two biblical sections, one of which is vastly more dramatic than the other: the tense, intriguing plot of 1 and 2 Samuel, and the more pedestrian detail of 1 Chronicles, which largely consists of preparation for temple worship. Yet in each case, the authors conclude with the focus on the house of God rather than the fights and betrayals. Exodus ends with the glory of God filling the tabernacle. Second Samuel ends with the purchase of the land on which the temple will be built. First Chronicles ends with a financial offering for the temple, and David's prayer of thanksgiving. It is as if the authors are saying that David and Moses saw rescue and failure, victory and loss. But more than anything else, they had a passion for the house of God.

And that is perhaps the most moving way in which King David serves as a prelude to King Jesus. We are probably used to seeing some of the parallels: David was sung about before he was born, anointed by the great prophet of his day, rejected by his brothers, triumphant in his fight against the great serpent on behalf of the nation, pursued and persecuted by the jealous king, repeatedly on the move with his band of not-so-merry men, and finally victorious in Jerusalem. Yet David's life, like Jesus's, was ultimately about the house of God. Picture David: leaving Jerusalem in another personal exodus, crossing the Kidron Valley and climbing up the Mount of Olives, weeping as he goes yet insisting that the ark of God be returned to the city (2 Sam. 15:19–31). He is betrayed by a close confidant, who later hangs himself (17:23). He is mocked and cursed, and when his friends try to fight for him, he rebukes them and takes the curses upon himself (16:5–14). Even after all this, his focus remains on the house of God: its location, materials, priests, musicians, gatekeepers, treasurers, architectural plans, and finances

(1 Chronicles 21–29). He is looking forward to the day when the kingdom will be fully established, the house of God dedicated, and the temple filled with glory. "Don't even think about leaving," he essentially tells his son Solomon, "until the temple is dedicated and the glory has come. It's all about the house."

Or, as Jesus will later put it, "Stay in the city until you are clothed with power from on high" (Luke 24:49). Don't even think about leaving until the temple is dedicated and the glory has come, complete with rushing wind and fiery tongues. It's all about the house.

Review Questions

1. Give some examples of echoes of exodus themes in David's psalms.
2. How are Goliath and Saul like Pharaoh?
3. How does David's story of leaving Jerusalem following Absalom's coup anticipate Christ's leaving Jerusalem?

Thought Questions

1. Can you identify some of the other biblical stories that 1 Samuel 19:11–17 recalls?
2. What are some of the resemblances between the story of David and the stories of Jacob and his sons?
3. Why might a battle against the Amalekites be significant?

14

The End of the Exodus?

1 Kings 6–13

One question we have not explored yet, but which is worth asking, is this: When did the exodus from Egypt finish? On the night of Passover? When the Israelites had crossed the Red Sea? When they received the law? At the death of Moses? After the crossing of the Jordan or the fall of Jericho? At the death of Joshua? When David became king? Never?

One answer suggests that the exodus ends much later than we usually think: "In the four hundred and eightieth year after the people of Israel came out of the land of Egypt, in the fourth year of Solomon's reign over Israel, in the month of Ziv, which is the second month, he began to build the house of the LORD" (1 Kings 6:1).[1] Three things strike us. First, the construction of Solomon's temple is dated from the exodus. Second, it starts exactly twelve generations (480 = 12 x 40) after Israel left Egypt. Third, when we add the time taken to build the temple (seven years) and the king's palace (thirteen years), it is exactly five hundred years from the Passover to the day Solomon blesses God for keeping his promise to Israel: "Blessed be the LORD who has given rest to his people Israel, according to all that he promised. Not one word has failed of all his good promise, which he spoke by Moses his servant" (1 Kings 8:56). The building of the temple, the dwelling place of God, somehow completes the exodus. The dream that had gripped the Israelites as they fled Egypt that night, with bowls of dough on their shoulders and anxious children in tow—the dream of being secure, prosperous, at peace, ruled by a wise king, and with a permanent house in which God's glory lives forever—has finally been realized.

It is hard for us to grasp the significance of the temple. Israel did not see it mainly as a structure, or even as a place to go and offer sacrifice; they saw it as the place where God came down to meet them, the meeting point of heaven and earth. That's why first the tabernacle, and then (more spectacularly) the temple, were filled with reminders of Eden, the place where God walked with humans.[2] In fact, the whole thing was built to suggest a fruitful, verdant, and well-watered garden.

A walk through the temple would reveal images of pomegranates, open flowers, palm trees, lilies, cedars, and olive wood. There were basins of water sitting on bronze stands with chariot wheels (which would have also reminded worshipers of the time they walked between walls of water, chased by chariot-riding Egyptians). There were two guarding cherubim in the inner room, images of cherubim on the walls and at the doors, and two huge bronze pillars guarding the entrance to the temple, all of which echo the cherubim set up as sentries at the entrance to the garden of Eden. The temple is even described as having a face, ribs, and shoulders (1 Kings 6:3, 5, 8; 7:39), which guide our minds back to the way Eve was "built" from Adam's rib in the garden. The temple is an architectural symbol of the bride that Solomon brings to the Lord. It is also, like Eden, a sanctuary where God would be especially present, and into which the riches of the nations would come—a pattern that begins almost immediately with the visit of the Queen of Sheba.

If only we could stop the story at 1 Kings 8. The temple is built and dedicated. The glory has come. Israel is settled, rich, peaceful, and happy. All the promises have come to pass. And they all lived happily ever after.

Except that they didn't, and those of us who have read exodus stories before will already know why. Solomon, like Adam and Israel before him, falls, and in doing so switches from being the heroic Joshua of this exodus story into being its tragic Pharaoh. He starts by marrying Pharaoh's daughter (1 Kings 9:16). Then he uses forced labor to complete building projects, like Pharaoh, and builds store cities, like Pharaoh (9:15–19). Then he builds a fleet and stations it on the Red Sea (9:26). He amasses horses from Egypt, chariots from Egypt, and gold (10:14–29). He worships false gods, building high places for idolatrous sacrifice (11:1–8). In an extraordinary echo of Exodus 1–2, Solomon even ends up opposed by a young man from another nation who was nearly killed at birth, but escaped to Egypt, ended up joining Pharaoh's family, asked for permission to leave, and then became an adversary (11:14–22). Solomon tries to kill the man he has placed in charge of the forced labor, Jeroboam, who flees to—you've guessed it—Egypt (11:26–40). By the time Solomon's son takes over the throne, the people are referring to Solomon as a king who "made our yoke heavy" and "disciplined . . . with whips" (12:10–11). The son of David has become the scourge of Israel. The seed of the woman has become the dragon.

Worse is to come. As an act of judgment on Solomon, God splits the kingdom into two: the southern two tribes under his son Rehoboam, and the northern ten tribes under Jeroboam. If we had any hope that this might put a stop to Israel's descent into idolatry, it is immediately dashed; Jeroboam becomes the new Aaron, setting up worship of not just one but two golden calves, and declaring, "Behold your gods, O Israel, who brought you up out of the land of Egypt" (1 Kings 12:28). He sets up a new priesthood for idolatrous worship, and even names his sons Nadab and Abijah (14:1, 20), just as Aaron named his boys Nadab and Abihu. Rehoboam fares no better; he is continuously at war with the northern tribes, and the king of (once again) Egypt comes up against him and plunders the temple. In the space of a few years, exodus triumph has become wilderness rebellion.

Yet the God of the exodus is still there. He remembers his covenant. And into this chaotic disintegration, this calamitous mess, he speaks. He raises up a man of God, a mini-Moses, to judge Jeroboam and promise the eventual destruction of idolatrous worship (1 Kings 13). This prophet from Judah, whose name we do not even know, confronts the king (as Moses did), confirms his word with a miraculous sign of judgment against him (as Moses did), sees the altar split (as the tablets of stone were split), and sees its ashes poured out (as the golden calf was ground to powder and poured out). More ominously, this prophet even gets distracted on his journey, disobeys God, and dies before he reaches his destination (as Moses did). But before he does, he speaks a word of judgment, which is also a word of promise: "O altar, altar, thus says the LORD: 'Behold, a son shall be born to the house of David, Josiah by name, and he shall sacrifice on you the priests of the high places who make offerings on you'" (13:2). Like Moses, this man of God can see a future in which God will once again act to deliver the nation by raising up a leader who will abandon foreign gods and unite the nation. It will take a while, though. Israel had to wait forty years for Joshua. She will have to wait nearly three hundred years for Josiah.

Six hundred years after Josiah, another prophet from Judah will come to Israel. He will confront the nation's rulers and speak judgment against their acts of worship, confirming his words with miraculous signs. He will turn over the temple tables, temporarily bringing the sacrificial system to a standstill, and denounce those who run it as a gang of robbers. He will also be ignored, killed, and buried in another man's grave. Like Jeroboam, Jerusalem's leaders will simply put all the tables back and carry on as normal, and as the man from Judah is killed by a lion, so the Lion of Judah will be killed by men.

What happens in death, however, makes all the difference. When Josiah finally fulfills this prophecy and destroys Jeroboam's altar, he finds the tomb of the prophet from Judah and insists that nobody move his bones (2 Kings 23:18). When they found the tomb of the prophet from Judea, on the other hand, there were no bones left to move.

Review Questions

1. How might the building of the temple be regarded as the completion of the exodus? How does it resemble Eden?
2. How does Solomon become like Pharaoh?
3. How does Israel's fall from the heights of the glories of Solomon's early reign echo earlier fall stories?

Thought Questions

1. How might the fact that Solomon is like a new Adam shed light upon his request for wisdom in 1 Kings 3? How might this inform our reading of Genesis 3?
2. How does Deuteronomy 17:14–17 bring Solomon's fall into clearer focus?
3. How might the peculiar story of 1 Kings 13 serve as a parable for the entire people's destiny?

15

Elijah and Elisha

1 Kings 16–2 Kings 13

The divided kingdom lasted three hundred and fifty years, a largely idolatrous roller coaster of (one or two) ups and (an awful lot of) downs, and the subject of most of 1 and 2 Kings. Yet for all the major events he has to cover in that time—the split under Rehoboam, the exile of the northern kingdom into Assyria, the restoration of the temple under Josiah, and especially the exile of the southern kingdom into Babylon—the author gives over half of his narrative to the period spanned by just two men: Elijah and Elisha. Clearly, this prophetic double act is hugely important. Why?

At first glance, we might think this was simply because their lives include so many dramatic stories. These nineteen chapters contain countless tales of droughts and downpours, earthquakes and hurricanes and still small voices, murders and battles, river crossings and optical illusions, fires and chariots and fiery chariots, whirlwinds and bears, oil and flour, axes and stews, sieges and famines, plots and assassinations, the healing of lepers, and the raising of the dead. But while this is true, it ignores the fact that the writer of 1 and 2 Kings doesn't seem to mind tedious lists—the continual cycle of kings falling into idolatry is repetitive and boring (partly because idolatry itself is repetitive and boring)—and it also avoids the question of *why* so many miracles and dramatic events happened through these two men. A better answer, which explains both the concentration of miracles and the focus of the writer, is that we have another exodus on our hands. Elijah is a new Moses. Elisha is a new Joshua.

It starts, as exoduses usually do, with the people of God suffering under the leadership of a Pharaoh-like figure. In this case, the part of Pharaoh is played by four kings and a queen: the Omride dynasty of Omri, Ahab and his wife Jezebel, and their sons Ahaziah and Jehoram. Under their appalling leadership, idolatry runs rife, Jericho is rebuilt, the righteous are oppressed, and Canaanite pagan worship is reinstated. Drought and famine strike the land. People are killed for prophesying. Naboth is falsely accused and then murdered simply for owning land that the king wanted to steal. Ahab in particular, we are told, "did more to provoke the LORD, the God of Israel, to anger than all the kings of Israel who were before him" (1 Kings 16:33), which, given the company he is in, is really saying something. The stage is set for another battle of the gods.

Up steps Elijah. The drought that he brings to the land, like the plagues Moses and Aaron bring upon Egypt, does not represent punishment as much as it demonstrates that the Lord is the true God and Baal is not. In this sense it functions like a three-year-long, national-scale version of the showdown at Mount Carmel. Baal and Asherah, the gods of Ahab and Jezebel, are supposed to be able to bring rain and fertility. But they are exposed as completely impotent; they cannot make a single drop of water fall, any more than they can bring fire out of the sky (which is why Elijah stopping the rain is the Canaanite equivalent of Aaron turning the river Nile to blood or Moses darkening the sun). Having brought the "plague" of drought, Elijah immediately leaves the land, heads east across the River Jordan, finds water in a dry place, and has bread and meat miraculously provided from the skies by ravens, before blessing a foreigner with both food and life. The echoes of the exodus are unmistakable.

The next two chapters unfold on two mountains, which evoke different aspects of Israel's encounters at Sinai. Mount Carmel, famously, is a mountain of confrontation, where Israel is confronted with the challenge to worship God alone, an altar is established, the living God descends in fire, idols are exposed as frauds, idol worshipers are killed, the people acknowledge the true God, and a meal is eaten.[1] Mount Horeb, by contrast, is a mountain of comfort: a place where Elijah, desiring to die and not having eaten for forty days and forty nights, is reassured by a direct encounter with the divine presence, and leaves with fresh impetus and faith to lead the nation. In the story of the great exodus, Mount Sinai—which, we should remember, is also called Mount Horeb—was both of these things at once, a place of judgment and blessing, confrontation and comfort. There may even be exodus significance in the fact that, sandwiched between these two mountain encounters, we have a story about a thick cloud descending, a king on a chariot (Ahab/Pharaoh) racing to escape stormy waters, and the man of God (Elijah/Moses) going ahead of him, carried by the hand of the Lord. Eventually Ahab, like Pharaoh, will die in his chariot, which will end up underwater (1 Kings 22:38).

It is at this point in each story that we first meet the prophetic successors, Joshua and Elisha. Both men have similar names, which highlight the rescue God will work through them: *Joshua* means "the Lord Saves," and *Elisha* means "God Saves." Both men will serve older leaders for some time, before being commissioned on the far side of the Jordan. Both will begin their leadership with a miraculous river crossing, in imitation of their mentors. Both will immediately face unanswered questions about the location of their predecessors' bodies. Both are called to take the land of Israel for the Lord, beginning in Jericho. Both will show unusual kindness to a person from an enemy nation (Rahab the Canaanite prostitute and Naaman the Syrian leper), bring judgment to Israelites who steal things (Achan and Gehazi), and conquer foreign armies in miraculous ways.

Perhaps the strangest thing that Moses and Joshua have in common with Elijah and Elisha, however, is that their exoduses never quite finish. Moses led Israel out of Egypt but died outside the land. Joshua led Israel into the Promised Land, but his campaign against idolatry and sin and his conquest of the land were left incomplete. Elijah and Elisha confronted and destroyed the Pharaoh-like Omride dynasty, with a bit of help from Jehu and the king of Syria, but Israel quickly tumbled back into idolatry and wickedness and was eventually deported a hundred years later. For all the miraculous provision of food and water, healing and life, their ultimate aim—the restoration of Israel—was never achieved.

That had to wait for another pair of prophets. The first, like Moses and Elijah, was a man of the wilderness, crying out for repentance and confronting the nation's wicked ruler. The second, like Joshua and Elisha, was commissioned at the Jordan, worked wonders, welcomed prostitutes and enemy soldiers, healed lepers, provided miraculous food for people, pronounced judgment on rebellious cities, and raised the dead to life. Like Joshua and Elisha, he carried salvation in his very name: *Yeshua*, or "the Lord Saves." Yet unlike them, he was able to bring about the great deliverance that Israel truly needed. "You shall call his name Jesus," the angel had told Joseph, "for he will save his people from their sins" (Matt. 1:21).

Review Questions

1. How does the relationship between Moses and Joshua help us to understand the relationship between Elijah and Elisha?
2. How can the exodus narrative help us to understand the significance of Elijah's journey to Mount Horeb?
3. How is Ahab like Pharaoh?

Thought Questions

1. Ahab wants to transform Naboth's vineyard into a vegetable garden. Why might this be significant (Deut. 11:10; Ps. 80:8)?
2. Why are miracles so concentrated in particular portions of biblical history, such as the stories of Elijah and Elisha, yet so rare elsewhere?
3. Identify some of the similarities between the miracles performed by Elisha and those performed by Christ. How might understanding both Elisha and Christ in relation to Joshua help us to appreciate the meaning of their ministries?

16

The Outstretched Arm

Isaiah–Malachi

People remember military victories in three main ways, although in the modern world we tend to express only two of them. The first is in celebration, or even nostalgia: we won, they lost, we're great, they're not, yah-boo-sucks. Trivial or not, this is the kind of memory reflected in Shakespeare's *Henry V*, Tchaikovsky's *1812 Overture*, the Arc de Triomphe and Trafalgar Square, Independence Day fireworks, and "The Star-Spangled Banner." The second is in regret or lament: yes, we prevailed, but the costs were so terrible that we must never, ever allow that to happen again. This is remembrance through memorial walls, poppies, "Anthem for Doomed Youth," "lest we forget," war cemeteries, and moments of silence. Both of these involve looking back, whether to learn lessons, honor sacrifice, or treasure national triumphs.

But there's a third way of remembering victory, and it's the way Israel reflects on the exodus from Egypt. As judgment falls on the nation for idolatry, with the northern and southern kingdoms imploding and exile approaching, the prophets keep calling Israel to remember the exodus—but not in nostalgia for a past golden age and certainly not in lament for tragedy, but in hope for the future. Israel worships the God of the exodus: the God who may appear silent but who hears the cry of his people, and who is quietly preparing to liberate them from captivity with a mighty hand and an outstretched arm. So when all seems lost, there is hope. The God of the exodus lives. He will redeem them. "It has happened before," you can imagine Charlton Heston gravely reminding the desperate nation, "and it will happen again. The only question is when."

The so-called minor prophets are continually pointing Israel forward by pointing them back, and to the exodus in particular. The turning point of Hosea, in which God erupts in love and compassion for Israel in spite of their whoredom and idolatry, is shot through with exodus imagery: "out of Egypt I called my son"; "I bent down to them and fed them"; "it was I who taught Ephraim to walk"; "they shall come trembling like birds from Egypt, . . . and I will return them to their homes" (Hos. 11:1–11). Joel celebrates Egypt's future desolation and Israel's future prosperity. Jonah, who knows a thing or two about the exodus-style mercy of God, having just experienced a journey into the waters and out again, gets frustrated with the Lord for forgiving Nineveh, and as he does so, he uses the very words God revealed to Moses on Sinai: "That is why I made haste to flee to Tarshish; for I knew that you are a gracious God and merciful, slow to anger and abounding in steadfast love" (Jon. 4:2). Micah refers to the same passage, and centers his appeal to Israel on the exodus, the leadership of Moses, Aaron, and Miriam, and the "righteous acts of the Lord" when God's people were threatened by Balak (Mic. 6:3–5; 7:15, 18–19). Habakkuk 3 is an extended reflection on the exodus. Zechariah promises

110

restoration in language that comes straight out of the Red Sea crossing (Zech. 10:8–12). It has happened before. It will happen again.

The writings of the major prophets are shaped by the exodus too, only at greater length. Jeremiah spends his entire ministry warning Judah that they are about to be taken captive into a foreign land, where they will need to settle in for the long haul and await the deliverance that the Lord will eventually bring. This deliverance will be so dramatic that people will no longer swear by the God who brought Israel out of Egypt but by the God who brought Israel out of exile (Jer. 16:14–15); not only that, but the covenant will not be like the exodus one, which Israel broke, but a new one in which, God says, "I will put my law within them, and I will write it on their hearts" (31:33). Daniel, who prophesies from within Babylon, is himself a sort of Joseph figure—a wise man who gains influence with the king by refusing to compromise morally, interpreting dreams and providing good counsel, to the extent that the king ends up worshiping Israel's God—although like Israel, Daniel also sees the transition to a new king, who does not know God and who will face judgment for his idolatrous ways (Daniel 1–5).

The exodus is even more prominent in the ministry of Ezekiel.[1] Like Moses, he receives a dramatic vision of God in fire, in an unexpected place (Ezekiel 1); he goes to speak to the captives of his people (3); and he is a Levite prophet, sent to a rebellious and idolatrous people with signs and with plagues (4–6), leading up to a Passover event (9). Like Moses, he is fundamentally a prophet of the divine presence, who sees that God is on the move and accompanies his people wherever they go (1; 10; 48). Like Moses, he is given instruction for proper worship. The book concludes on a high mountain, where Ezekiel is given a law and instructions for feasts, and from which he surveys the ordering of the temple, the city, and the entire land (40–48). The three major sections of his book are exodus-shaped as well. In the first part (1–24), as Ezekiel preaches judgment on Israel, the exodus story is central to his savage rebuke of the nation's idolatry (16; 20; 23). In the second (25–32), as he preaches judgment on the surrounding nations, by far the longest section is devoted to Egypt and Pharaoh (29–32). And the third section (33–48) pivots on an act of grace in which the Lord will take Israel out of captivity, cleanse them from idolatry, give them a new heart, bring them into their own land, and fill them with his Spirit (36–37). The echoes of the exodus here are as loud and clear as anywhere else in the Prophets—except, that is, for Isaiah.

Isaiah's rich and beautiful prophecy contains a dramatic exodus triple-whammy, as he promises first rescue from Assyria, then redemption from Babylon, and finally redemption from sin itself, in a fashion that echoes the exodus but turns it completely on its head. (If you've ever seen pianists cross their hands midway through a piece, you know how strange it is to hear the same notes being played, as it were, upside down. That, as we will see, is what happens in Isaiah 51–55.)

In the first half of Isaiah, the shape of Israel's deliverance is familiar. There is a Pharaoh figure, the king of Assyria, who thinks he is stronger than the Lord and is keen to oppress God's people, but who (it turns out) is being used by God to achieve his purposes. There is the assurance that God will come down in fire, that the Assyrians will be first struck with plagues and then wiped out in one day, and that Israel will be rescued, return to their land by crossing a river on dry land, and sing the song of Exodus 15 on the far side (Isaiah 10–12). There is the promise of tragedy upon the unbelieving city and judgment upon the dragon that is in the sea, while God's people are brought back from Egypt and ascend his mountain to eat and drink with him (24–27). So when we finally meet Sennacherib, king of Assyria, we already know what will happen. We find a threat to God's people, trash talk from the enemy, false promises, and desperate prayer to the God of heaven's armies. And then it happens. The angel of the Lord goes out, at night, and strikes down the Assyrians by the thousands. The world's most powerful empire is defeated in twelve hours, along with their gods, and Israel wakes in the morning to find their salvation has been accomplished without their having lifted a finger (36–37). The God of the exodus lives. His people are free.

But not for long. Just over a century later, Babylon will play the role of Egypt, and Judah will once again be in captivity to a foreign power, banished to a foreign land, and surrounded by foreign gods. So another exodus is needed, one in which God redeems his people from slavery, exposes the impotence of idols, releases prisoners from bondage, dries up the rivers and makes a way through the sea, provides water to the thirsty from a rock in the wilderness, and enables Israel to flee in joy, saying "The LORD has redeemed his servant Jacob!" (Isa. 48:20; see Isaiah 40–48). Babylon and its gods will come to nothing. Israel will be free.

But not for long. And this is where Isaiah starts to turn everything on its head, playing the same notes but crossing his hands over. Judah's problem, we discover, is deeper than physical captivity and harder to crack than mere armies. They are captive to sin itself: their iniquity, their faithlessness, their tendency to revert to idolatry even after they have been rescued again and again. In their captivity, they are inclined to think that God has forgotten them. Yet as with Israel's oppression in Egypt, the Lord remembers: "Can a woman forget her nursing child, that she can have no compassion on the son of her womb? Even these may forget, yet I will not forget you. Behold, I have engraved you on the palms of my hands" (Isa. 49:15–16). With exodus imagery pouring forth—"O arm of the LORD; awake. . . . Was it not you who cut Rahab in pieces, who pierced the dragon? Was it not you who dried up the sea, the waters of the great deep, who made the depths of the sea a way for the redeemed to pass over?" (Isa. 51:9–10)—we anticipate a new act of deliverance, not just temporarily from the latest invader, but once and for all (49–51).

The arm of the Lord, as we know by now, is about strength, power, even violence: the mighty hand and the outstretched arm that rain hailstones like fists and split the ocean. So as Isaiah begins to celebrate Judah's redemption, we are not surprised to hear that it comes about because "the LORD has bared his holy arm before the eyes of all nations," and that his servant will be "high and lifted up" (Isa. 52:10, 13). Here it comes: the violent showdown we have all been waiting for. We can hear Wagner's *Ride of the Valkyries* beginning in the background.

But the orchestra goes silent. Suddenly, the concert hall is deathly quiet. No trumpets or horns sound; the strings are muffled, and the oboes have been gently put back on the floor. The only sound we can hear is a plaintive cry, and as we peer at the stage in astonishment, we notice that it is coming from a manger, or the graveside of a friend, or a hillside garden, or even a cross. It is the cry of one like a root out of dry ground, with no beauty that we should desire him, despised and rejected by men, a man of sorrows and acquainted with grief (Isa. 53:2–3). Here, we learn, is what the arm of the Lord actually looks like in person: one who bears our griefs, carries our sorrows, is pierced for our transgressions, and is crushed for our iniquities (53:5). That is how Israel will be accounted righteous. That is what causes barren women to burst into song and thirsty travelers from every nation to descend on Jerusalem for a free banquet (53–55).

We didn't think the new exodus would look like that at all. We were so busy looking for God in the plagues or chariots hurled into the sea that we missed him in the fragile baby drifting downstream in a basket, and in the lamb's blood smeared across the doorpost, and in the two goats who face death and exile to take away the sins of the people. The God of the exodus is still high and lifted up, and he still redeems with a mighty hand and an outstretched arm. But now he is high and lifted up on a cross, and his arms are outstretched sideways, and his mighty hands have nails in them. Isaiah is as surprised as anyone: "Who has believed what he has heard from us? And to whom has the arm of the LORD been revealed?" (Isa. 53:1). Who indeed?

Review Questions

1. How does the exodus serve as a source of hope? Give some examples of the prophets' use of the exodus in this way.
2. How does the exodus provide the background for the coming new covenant?
3. How is Ezekiel like a new Moses?

Thought Questions

1. How can the prophets' use of the exodus story inform a "figural" or "musical" reading of Scripture?
2. How does Isaiah relate the exodus to creation themes (Isa. 51:12–16; 63:11–14)?
3. How do the prophets disclose the role of the Spirit in fulfilling the exodus?

17

Purim and Purity

Ezra–Esther

In many ways, the last history books of the Old Testament could hardly be more different. Ezra-Nehemiah, which in the Hebrew Bible was all on one scroll, reads like a detailed—even slightly pedantic—national history, complete with lists, names, numbers, official documents, and building projects. It is based in Israel, entirely about men, focused on the worship of God, largely humorless (unless you count that bit when Nehemiah matter-of-factly says, "I . . . beat some of them and pulled out their hair," Neh. 13:25), and ends in disappointment, as the Israelites continue to marry foreign women. Esther, on the other hand, is a gripping story of heroism, dramatic irony, clownish villains, and poetic justice. It is set in Persia, never specifically mentions God, revolves around a beautiful and courageous woman, ends in triumph, and reads like a pantomime, with a fair maiden, a boorish king, an evil prime minister who gets booed every time he steps on stage, and Mordecai as Buttons, the British panto-mime figure. The narrative high point of Ezra-Nehemiah is when a wall gets completed. The high point of Esther involves a tense nighttime confrontation, an enemy getting hoisted by his own petard, and a nation being saved from slaughter. Again: apples and oranges.

These very different histories have at least one thing in com-mon, however: they both echo the exodus. Together they tell the story of Israel being dramatically freed from foreign oppressors and their gods, against all the odds and in the face of fierce op-position, and being released to go and worship the Lord, follow his laws, and enter his land. The story of Esther, which chrono-logically happens first, has more in common with the first half of Exodus; Ezra-Nehemiah has more in common with the second. Yet each book draws attention to the great deliverance God has brought about and the need for Israel to respond in faithfulness.

The book of Esther begins in a way that should be famil-iar by now. The Israelites are under the rule of a foreign em-pire (Persia/Egypt). A previous king had shown favor to them (Cyrus/Pharaoh), even to the point of giving them their own portion of land (Susa/Goshen), partly through the wisdom of a young man who had great wisdom in interpreting dreams (Daniel/Joseph). But now we hear that a new king is on the throne (Xerxes/Pharaoh), and he is an ungodly and arrogant fool. Then, in Esther 2, we meet the one through whom God will rescue his people (Esther/Moses): a young person of beauty, who through the wisdom of her relative (Mordecai/Miriam) ends up being brought into the king's family. We have been here before.

The next chapter introduces us to the serpent figure, Haman, who is an Agagite. This in itself tells us something: the Agagites were descended from Agag the Amalekite, the king whom Saul had been commanded to destroy (1 Samuel 15), because the Amalekites had opposed Israel as they fled from Egypt. From an Israelite perspective, to be an Agagite is to be an enemy. So we are not surprised when Haman reacts with fury to Mordecai and seeks to destroy all the Jews. This move, from jealousy to hatred to attempted genocide, began with Pharaoh, but has tragically played itself out repeatedly in history, from Haman to Herod to Hitler.

Having said that, if we read the story through an exodus lens, we do not merely know that there will be an attempt to oppress and destroy Israel; we also know that the attempt will fail. What is more, we know *how* it will fail. It will involve the serpent being deceived by the shrewdness of the righteous (repeatedly, in fact, as in a farcical turn of events Haman ends up publicly honoring his enemy Mordecai, and then being tricked and outmaneuvered by the queen). It will include the poetic justice of seeing Israel's enemy having the tables turned on him, in this case hanging on the gallows he had intended for the Jews, much as Egypt had drowned in the sea after trying to drown the Israelite boys. The turning point will be a nighttime meal, in which the judgment of death—which was decreed on the day before Passover (Est. 3:12)—will pass from Israel to their enemies (7:1–10). Israel will end up with spoil from the very enemies who were trying to kill them (9:1–10) and security in the land. The whole episode will be commemorated with a feast and a holiday from that day forward (9:23–38). Echoes of the exodus are everywhere.

One more aspect of the Esther story is worth noticing, although it is one that has more to do with a future exodus than a past one. On hearing the decree, given just before Passover, that her people are about to be destroyed, Esther calls the Jews to fast for three days and nights (Est. 4:16). Following this period of prayer, she will approach the king to see if he will extend his scepter toward her and grant her request; as she points out to Mordecai, she is as good as dead if he doesn't (4:11). On the third day, she finds favor in the king's sight and is raised up, as if from death, and given whatever she asks for (5:1–3). She asks for the deliverance of her people. That marvelous cycle of prayer, death, third-day resurrection, and the redemption of a people, as we know, will be back.

Most of the events of Ezra-Nehemiah take place a generation later, and their echoes of the exodus are somewhat different. Both Ezra and Nehemiah begin with stories about Israelites being given permission by the Persian king to return to their land, so in a sense we are beginning the exodus story halfway through (although note that both Cyrus and Artaxerxes give permission more readily than Pharaoh!).[1] In Ezra, we hear about offerings being taken for the temple, including contributions from Gentiles, a numbering of the people, the reestablishment of Mosaic worship, the completion of the temple, and the celebration of the Passover. Nehemiah, likewise, focuses on a building project—in this case the walls of Jerusalem—and the obligations of the Mosaic covenant, including a climactic celebration of the Feast of Tabernacles, as Israel did in the wilderness. Both books, in that sense, tell the same story as the second half of Exodus and the book of Numbers.

Ezra and Nehemiah are also filled with stories of opposition, which remind us of Israel's wandering in the wilderness. Sometimes this opposition comes from within God's people, through covenant faithlessness and banned sexual relationships. Sometimes it comes from outside it, as the people of the land do their best to scupper Israel's chances. Most of us, if we're honest, find neither Numbers nor Ezra-Nehemiah the easiest parts of Scripture to read, but the light they shed on the journey of God's people is remarkable: alongside the obvious difficulties of persecution and confrontation (whether from Edomites, Moabites, Ammonites, or whomever), we all face the more subtle challenges of disillusionment, immorality, idolatry, and fear. Scripture and history are full of people who could withstand an army, but crumbled in the face of sexual temptation or a golden calf.[2]

119

In response to this opposition, Ezra serves as a new Moses. He is committed to studying, observing, and teaching the law, he urges Israel to keep God's covenant, and he prays for them to be forgiven when they don't. Nehemiah, whose account of the exodus story is one of the longest in the whole Bible (Nehemiah 9), might remind us of Phinehas, whose zeal for the law led to drastic action when he saw God's people compromising with foreign women (though the fact that Nehemiah "beat some of them and pulled out their hair" looks rather mild in comparison to spearing a couple while they are having sex!). Yet Ezra-Nehemiah ends in disappointment. Israel is in the land geographically, but the promises of inheritance, renewal, and blessing have not come to pass. It is as if this exodus story ends where Deuteronomy finished, with the death of Moses, a song of warning, and the Israelites stranded on the plains of Moab.

This is no accident. As the history of the Old Testament draws to a close, we are still waiting for a new Joshua, who will lead Israel into the fullness of their inheritance, cleanse their land, and conquer their enemies. Only then will Israel's exile be truly over, their return to the land complete, and their exodus fully accomplished.

Review Questions

1. How does the beginning of the book of Esther echo the beginning of the book of Exodus?
2. Identify some of the ways in which Ezra resembles Moses.
3. What are some of the chief struggles Ezra and Nehemiah faced? Compare and contrast these with the struggles Moses and earlier leaders faced.

Thought Questions

1. How can reading the Bible musically help us to answer those who might doubt that God is really present and active in Esther, as he isn't explicitly mentioned?

2. How does the recounting of Israel's history in Nehemiah 9 reveal the Jews' understanding of their situation relative to the exodus?

3. How does the conclusion of Nehemiah resemble a fall narrative? How does this color our understanding of the return?

FOURTH MOVEMENT

• • • •

THE GREAT
DELIVERANCE

18

The Crescendo

Matthew–John

The life of Jesus is an exodus, hidden in plain sight.

It starts with the nativity. The homespun charm of the Christmas story and the sentimentality with which we often celebrate it can obscure the exodus music that reverberates through it, even for those who know the story well. Matthew and Luke do their utmost to help us hear it, though. At times, the familiar rhythms and melodies become almost deafening.

Take an example that most of us miss: the names of the characters. We know this is an exodus story as soon as we are introduced to the cast. We have a Joseph, a faithful Israelite who has dreams and receives promises of God's miraculous redemption to come. We have an Elisheba (Elizabeth), the wife of the priest from the family of Aaron (Ex. 6:23). We have a Miriam (Mary), the courageous woman who becomes a mother to God's people by protecting the promised rescuer in childhood, and who sings prophetically of God's mighty act of deliverance. We have a Hannah (Anna), the faithful woman who prays in the temple for the redemption of Israel, recognizes the miracle child as God's answer, and proclaims it to the world. We have men whose names witness to the fact that God hears the cry of his people and remembers them: Zacharias ("the LORD Remembers") and Simeon ("Heard"). And we have the one for whom the whole nation has been waiting: a Joshua (Jesus).

The exodus and nativity stories are, in outline, remarkably similar. We start with Israel being oppressed by a foreign power, women of faithfulness and bravery, the birth of a male child, and an evil king intent on destroying him by killing baby boys. We have an angelic appearance to a shepherd or shepherds, with the promise of a "sign" that will demonstrate that God's word has been fulfilled. Signs appear in the night sky. Gentiles give gifts and come to worship Israel's God. The chosen people escape in response to a nighttime angelic encounter, before waiting and then reentering the land. The striking difference is that while Israel escapes from Egypt into the land, Jesus escapes from the land into Egypt. But as Matthew points out, Jesus is identifying with Israel in his journey into Egypt and then out again; the prophecies of both Hosea and Jeremiah, originally given about Israel's departure and return, now apply to Jesus as the new Israel.[1] The Israel musical theme is being taken up and incorporated into the Jesus theme.

Intriguingly, even the Gospels without a nativity story draw our attention to the exodus as they introduce Jesus. For John, the birth of Jesus is the moment when "the Word became flesh and dwelt [or *tabernacled*] among us," revealing the glory of God which nobody has ever seen and bringing a fresh revelation of grace and truth on top of that which came through Moses (1:14–18). The echoes of Exodus 32–34 could hardly be clearer. For Mark, John the Baptist is like the angel of the Lord who goes before Israel. "Behold, I send my messenger before your face"

(Mark 1:2) is very close to Exodus 23:20, which indicates both that God's forerunner (John/the angel) is preparing the way for his chosen one (Jesus/Israel) and that the journey ahead will be perilous, filled with opposition, and in need of angelic protection. As Mark bombards us with stories of casting out demons and sicknesses and cleansing the land from hostile powers who know Jesus has come to destroy them, we remember the way the Canaanites responded to Israel on hearing they were coming.[2]

So when Jesus's public ministry begins, we are expecting to hear about a forty-day (or year) time of testing in the wilderness and a crossing of the River Jordan. Jesus, like Israel, goes through the waters of baptism. He is given a physical representation of the Holy Spirit's presence with him—the dove reminds us both of Noah and of the Spirit hovering over the waters in creation—and he hears a voice from heaven announcing his identity and calling for the nation to listen. His baptism marks the transfer of leadership from John to Jesus, as it did from Moses to Joshua and from Elijah to Elisha; as he comes up out of the Jordan, he emerges with a new commission to move through the land and drive out the powers of darkness.

At the same time, like Israel, Jesus has a lengthy period of wandering in the desert. The Spirit leads him into a dry and barren place, in which he has to trust God for the provision of bread, resist evil, and stand on the testimony of Scripture. The specific temptations echo those that unraveled Israel: grumbling about the lack of food, testing God by demanding a miracle, bowing down to false gods, and seizing his inheritance before it was time. (It is no coincidence that in all three of his temptations Jesus quotes Deuteronomy, the sermon Moses preached to remind Israel of their need for obedience.) But Jesus succeeds where Israel failed. For all our familiarities with the exodus story in Scripture, we have never seen this before. The all-too-familiar biblical melody of failure has been transformed and turned into a song of hope.

When Jesus returns from the wilderness in Matthew, he calls disciples, much as Moses set up elders of the people in Exodus 18. He is followed by multitudes, goes up a mountain, and teaches people from it, much as Moses did. His teaching explores what it means to obey the law, just like Moses's did, although unlike Moses he teaches on his own authority and insists on a greater level of righteousness than was achievable through the law. Jesus identifies the people as "sheep without a shepherd" (Matt. 9:36) and immediately appoints leaders who will help them, just as Moses did with Joshua.[3] He sets apart twelve individuals and sends them into the land, as if to "spy it out" for the conquest of the gospel, just as Moses did. Those that receive these men will receive blessing—just as Rahab did—but those that reject them will face destruction, just as Ai did. Later on Jesus expands the group of leaders to seventy, just as Moses did.

Jesus identifies himself as the one who has not come to bring peace but a sword (Matt. 10:34), which suggests that in the person of Jesus, Joshua and the "commander of the LORD's army" have become one and the same (see Josh. 5:14).[4] He announces that the walls of the temple will come crashing down when the trumpets announce his coming, just as the walls of Jericho crumbled. Even his final words in Matthew, the so-called Great Commission, reflect God's commission to Joshua: I have given you everywhere you put your feet, to the very ends of the land. You are to obey whatever I commanded you. And I will be with you always.

The extent of all these exodus parallels—or, to return to our musical analogy, the volume at which the exodus theme is transposed, amplified, and turned into the Jesus theme—indicates that we are entering the final movement. As we have seen throughout this book, exodus echoes are everywhere, and they recapitulate and reinforce each other. In the person of Jesus, however, things are building toward a climax. The whole orchestra has been brought in. Choirs have been added. The music of the previous movements, from Abraham to Moses to Elijah and Elisha, is being drawn together into one magnificent harmony in a way that neglects none of them and transcends all of them. Listening for this helps us see not just what the exodus is about, but what the gospel of the kingdom is about.

Nowhere is this clearer than in the Gospel of John, which brings the exodus theme to a crescendo. Jesus is the provider of wine for God's people so they can celebrate with him, behold him, and eat and drink (John 2; cf. Exodus 24). He is the preacher of the new birth, through the waters and by the Spirit, and the bronze serpent lifted up in the wilderness, that whoever believes may have life (3). He is the fountain of water in dry places (4; 7). He heals those who have been weak and paralyzed, hopeless and lost—one man for thirty-eight years—and gives them rest (5; cf. Deut. 2:14). He provides the bread of heaven and reveals his sovereignty over the waters (6). He is the prophet like Moses and the source of true spiritual food and drink (6; 7). He is the light that leads Israel, the truth that liberates them from slavery, and the "I AM" of the burning bush (8). He is the shepherd who leads his people out and protects them (10). He turns Pharaoh's plagues on their heads, bringing fresh water to the thirsty, healing to those plagued with sickness, light in the darkness, and life to the dead, ultimately through his self-sacrifice as the King's firstborn Son at Passover. He is the true tabernacle, in whom we see what God truly looks like; the true mediator, who prays that his people would be united in truth and holiness; the true Lamb of God, who takes away the sin of the world.

Come, let us adore him.

Review Questions

1. How does the early ministry of Jesus from his baptism follow the pattern of Moses?
2. How is the Great Commission like Moses's charge to Joshua?

3. What are some of the images drawn from the exodus in the Gospel of John?

Thought Questions

1. How does the Passover-time story of the boy Jesus in Luke 2:41–50 anticipate his later story?
2. How do the "musical" details of John the Baptist's ministry (his clothing, his activity, his location, his self-descriptions, etc.) help us to understand the meaning of Jesus's ministry?
3. How is the story of Ezekiel 1–3 present in the background of Luke's account of Jesus's baptism, temptations, and preaching in Nazareth?

19

The Exodus of Jesus

Matthew–John

After numerous chapters of hint and suggestion, allusion and parallel, Luke finally gives it to us straight: Jesus is going to have an exodus of his own. This truth comes out on the Mount of Transfiguration: "And behold, two men were talking with him, Moses and Elijah, who appeared in glory and spoke of his *exodos*, which he was about to accomplish at Jerusalem" (Luke 9:30–31). Translate that word how you will—departure, exit, decease, death, exodus—but in New Testament times *exodos* was the word used to describe Israel's exodus from Egypt. And here we have Jesus talking—to Moses and Elijah no less—about how he is going to accomplish one in Jerusalem.

The exodus music in the Gospels has been building for a while, but as the transfiguration approaches, it becomes unmistakable. Jesus and the disciples have been working miracles, which have caught the attention of the Pharaoh-like Herod—

who, like Joseph's Pharaoh in Genesis 40:20–22, had just celebrated his birthday with an execution.[1] Jesus departs, crossing the sea, and heads out into the wilderness. He is followed by a multitude of Israelites who have no food, so Jesus delegates authority to his disciples (as did Moses), gets them arranged in groups of fifty (as did Moses), and provides heavenly bread for all of them (as did Moses). The parallels extend to the oddest of details, like the fact that only the men are numbered, and that there are twelve baskets of food left over. One for each tribe, presumably.

Eight days later—and frequently in Scripture, the eighth day is the day of new creation—Jesus goes up the mountain to pray, accompanied by Peter, James, and John, just as Moses had gone up Mount Sinai with Aaron, Nadab, and Abihu. The disciples see a theophany, an appearance of God, as the glory cloud descends. Central to the appearance is the transfiguration of Jesus's face, which is a fascinating detail since the "face" of God is precisely the part of him that Moses was *not* allowed to see. This, clearly, is a greater kind of theophany. Moses appears, along with Elijah, and Jesus talks with them about his *exodos*. Peter, worried that Moses and Elijah are about to leave, asks to prepare tents for everybody. If we have followed the story so far, we will roll our eyes at Peter here ("not knowing what he said," Luke 9:33), because we understand that Moses and Elijah, representing the Law and the Prophets, were always supposed to make way for the glory of Jesus, like John the Baptist becoming less so that Jesus might become greater. We will also notice the reference to tents (or tabernacles).

A voice from heaven is heard, proclaiming the identity of God's chosen One and urging people to listen to him, just as the Lord's descent on Mount Sinai validated the teaching of Moses through the law. Both Jesus and Moses encounter a multitude after coming down from the mountain, as well as representatives who have proved faithless in their task during their absence. The disciples have been unable to restrain a demon, who throws a boy down and "shatters him" (Luke 9:39), just as Aaron was unable to restrain demon worshipers, causing Moses to throw the tablets down and shatter them. Jesus rebukes the people fiercely: "O faithless and twisted generation, how long am I to be with you and bear with you?" (9:41). This, like so much of the passage, reminds us of the way Moses spoke about Israel in the wilderness: "They are a perverse generation, children in whom is no faithfulness" (Deut. 32:20).

All of this indicates that the *exodos* of Jesus is not just about his death, as the word *departure* might suggest, but about his glory, authority, revelation, life, death, resurrection, and ascension. Jesus is not just leaving. He is starting an exodus: a long-awaited escape from the land of slavery into a new world flowing with milk and honey, in which the slave masters are thrown down and drowned in the sea, but the multitude of faith, both Jew and Gentile, find freedom.

The escape theme comes through in some surprising ways. In his final few days, Jesus tells various stories about being ready and watchful because a nighttime flight is approaching rapidly. In Luke 17, as he is describing the coming of the Son of Man, he uses two exodus stories to encourage faith and warn about the consequences of turning back. The "days" of the Son of Man will be just like the "days" of Noah, when the enemies of God were drowned in water, and the "days" of Lot, when plagues from the sky brought destruction on a wicked city. Understandably, when telling the exodus story, we prefer to focus on what happened to Israel rather than what happened to Egypt, on Noah rather than the sons of Cain, on Lot rather than Sodom. But Jesus urged his disciples to learn from both—to resolve, as the old song has it, "to follow Jesus, no turning back, no turning back." Israel looked back, and they lost their inheritance. Lot's wife turned back, and she turned into a pillar of salt.

The model of resilience, of a steadfast commitment to leave

slavery behind and press on toward the promised inheritance, is Jesus himself. On the night he is betrayed, he enacts a mini-exodus of his own. After a Passover meal, at night, he leaves the city that is about to face judgment, followed by the Twelve (who represent the twelve tribes of Israel), crosses the river, and heads for the mountain where he meets with God, accompanied by angels. In doing so, Jesus also echoes the exodus of David after Absalom's coup: betrayed by a close friend and advisor (Judas, like Ahithophel), leaving Jerusalem and weeping, climbing the Mount of Olives, ministered to by a messenger (angels, like Ziba), assaulted with violence and cursing by enemies (soldiers, like Shimei), and with a right-hand man who wishes to strike them down (Peter, like Abishai), which he prevents.[2] Perhaps the most astonishing echo of the exodus in the betrayal story, and certainly the most puzzling for the people who experienced it, is the moment when Jesus says, "I am," and the soldiers draw back and fall to the ground (John 18:6). Jesus is Moses and Israel and David—but he is also the Lord, the God of the burning bush, in human form.

Not to mention that Jesus is the Passover Lamb. As each Gospel has emphasized in its own way, Jesus is pure and spotless, without blemish or fault. He offers himself over the Passover weekend. His death is a sacrifice that will ransom his people and substitute for the nation. The crucial meal involves his body being eaten by his followers. Not one of his bones is broken. Darkness covers the skies in the middle of the day, and then he dies. As he does so, his blood redeems first Jews, some of whom literally come out of their graves then and there, and then an untold multitude of Gentiles who join God's people in fleeing the slavery of sin and death—previously guilty criminals who, like Barabbas, started the day in prison expecting execution, and ended it with the jail doors wide open because an innocent One had become their substitute. Israel sacrificed a Passover lamb so as not have to sacrifice their firstborn sons. God, who is rich in mercy, sacrificed both.

The exodus of Israel did not finish in one night, as we know. Freedom, as Moses explained to Pharaoh, was three days' journey away, and was ultimately seen not in the escape at night, but as dawn broke in the morning and God's people saw their enemies lying vanquished in the deep. In the same way, it is at dawn on the third day, as the sun (and the Son) rises, that the tears of mourning turn to joy, and the temporary escape becomes a permanent deliverance, and the dragon is crushed, never to enslave again. "Why do you seek the living among the dead? He is not here, but has risen!" (Luke 24:5–6). Fittingly, it is once again Mary, or Miriam, who leads the women in celebration of the *exodos*.

The gospel story ends, if it ends at all, on a mountain. In Matthew it is a Joshua-like mountain, as Jesus commissions his followers to teach his commandments to all generations and go in to inherit the land he has secured for them, in confident knowledge of his presence. In Luke-Acts it is more of a Moses-like mountain, involving an ascension, a cloud, angels, shining clothes, and the instruction to wait for the Holy Spirit to fill his temple. Both of these Gospel writers, like the makers of *The Prince of Egypt*, conclude their exodus narratives on mountain-tops, and you can see why: the encounter with the Lord at Sinai is, in many ways, the climactic moment to which the rest of the story has been pointing. When we think of Jesus's ascension into heaven, when he is finally "lifted up from the earth" (John 12:32), seated at the right hand of the Father, and begins to draw all men to himself, we could say the same.

Yet even so, in all four Gospels, the story remains unfinished. The kingdom is not yet fully here. The Land has not yet been taken. The Spirit has not yet come. The exodus of Jesus may be over, but the exodus of his people has only just started.

Review Questions

1. Identify some of the exodus themes in the Gospel stories of the feeding of the five thousand.

2. How does the story of the exodus help us to understand the meaning of the transfiguration?
3. How do Jesus's death and resurrection take the form of an exodus?

Thought Questions

1. Who are the key Pharaoh figures in the Gospels? Is there an Ahab figure?
2. What are some of the ways in which the exodus stories of Elijah and Elisha serve as a background for the Gospel accounts of Christ? Having read Luke 4:24–27, compare Luke 7:1–10 and 7:11–17 with 2 Kings 5:1–19 and 1 Kings 17:17–24.
3. How does Jesus's exodus fulfill the meaning of earlier exoduses?

20

Sinai and Pentecost

Acts

What goes up must come down. The earthly ministry of Jesus culminates in his going up: up to Jerusalem, up to Skull Hill, up onto the cross, up from death to life, up to the Mount of Olives, and finally up into heaven. But the story of the gospel, Luke explains, is only what Jesus *began* to do and teach (Acts 1:1). The next part of his activity on earth, which Luke focuses on in Acts, will take place through the church, and it involves a coming down.

The gift of the Spirit at Pentecost is often associated with Babel, and with good reason. People are not scattering; God comes down and works a miracle of language; people scatter throughout the world; and the fulfillment of God's promise to Abraham begins. At Babel, this scattering was an act of judgment in response to disobedience, bringing incomprehension and fracture. At Pentecost, it is an act of blessing in response to obedience, bringing new understanding and unity. Pentecost, in an important sense, is Babel's reversal.

Yet Pentecost also echoes the exodus, and particularly the encounter on the mountain at Sinai. Some of these echoes are obvious. The law was given to Israel about seven weeks after the Passover; the Spirit is given to the church about seven weeks after the cross. The anointed leader has gone up, and the divine presence comes down. There are tangible physical signs: a great noise from heaven, whether thunder and trumpets or a mighty rushing wind, and the descent of God in fire. The gift that defines God's people—first the law and then the Spirit—is given. The people are commissioned as kings and priests, and the tabernacle/temple is established. A sermon is preached, calling for obedience. A new covenant has started.

Then there are subtler echoes, which indicate that Pentecost is in some ways the reversal of Sinai, as well as of Babel. Sinai was a moment of national apostasy. Moses came down the mountain to find the people embroiled in the most wicked act in their short history, worshiping a golden calf and thanking it for leading them out of slavery. God condemned them as a stiff-necked generation. Three thousand people were cut down by the sword, and died. From that time on, the promise of priesthood was limited to the Levites, who responded to the Lord's call.

Pentecost, on the other hand, is a moment of national blessing. Peter confronts the people after the most wicked act in their history, the crucifixion of their Messiah. Yet his confrontation is shot through with mercy. He promises forgiveness and the gift of the Holy Spirit. Instead of condemning them as a wicked generation, he offers them the chance to save themselves from a wicked generation. Three thousand people are cut to the heart by the word, and saved. From that time on, the promise is for all God's people, who respond to his call.

When you press in to take hold of your inheritance, however, you face opposition. Both Israel and the early church, as they begin to obey their God-given commission to "go into all the land/earth, for I am with you," have to face enemies from outside. This is to be expected: the powers-that-be are not impressed to hear that their time is up. But in both cases, these external enemies are not the real problem. The Sanhedrin is no more able to stop Peter and John than the Amalekites or the Canaanites were able to stop Joshua and Caleb; swords and spears, beatings and prison sentences, are no match for the prayers of God's people. The real problem comes from within. It comes from sexual immorality, pride, idol worship, injustice.

So it is tragic, if predictable, to read that just as the victories of Israel were marred by the greed of Achan, so the progress of the church was marred by the greed of Ananias and Sapphira (Josh. 7:1–26; Acts 5:1–10). Achan's greed is simple theft whereas Ananias and Sapphira's is exaggeration, but the root problem is the same. Joshua and Peter, respectively, express amazement that people could sin in such ways, given all the blessings they have received. And then comes the shocking bit: both families are singled out by the Lord, rebuked, and publicly killed, to cleanse the people and cause them to fear. As hard as we may find these stories to read, they point to the reality that, as Jesus explained, it is the inside rather than the outside of the cup that makes it unclean. More people die of infectious diseases than in warfare. More churches are undone by sin than by persecution. If God sees fit to use the ultimate sanction in response—and we should notice that God strikes Ananias and Sapphira directly, rather than telling the church to do it—it simply shows us the terrible severity of unrepentant sin.

Despite this, the Word of the Lord continues to grow and increase, just as Israel had in Egypt. And frequently, key breakthroughs come in exodus-shaped ways. After the Sadducees throw the apostles in prison, "during the night an angel of the Lord opened the prison doors and brought them out" (Acts 5:19). An argument about food is followed by new layers of delegated leadership. The sermons of Stephen (in Jerusalem) and Paul (in Pisidian Antioch) are chock-full of references to the exodus. Philip liberates a city with miracles, confronts the magician who was bamboozling the people, and then overtakes a chariot-riding African in the wilderness and immerses him in the waters. In this he imitates not only Moses, but also Elijah (1 Kings 18). Saul starts off as a Pharaoh-like figure, oppressing and persecuting the people of God, but is commissioned into a new Moses: he sees God's glory, and then is called twice by name ("Saul, Saul," echoing "Moses, Moses"), called to prevent the oppression of God's people, and sent before rulers to bring them into their inheritance. There are three stories of Moses seeing the glory of God in Exodus; this may explain why there are three stories of Paul seeing the glory of God in Acts (Ex. 3:1–6; 24:9–18; 33:12–34:9; Acts 9:1–9; 22:6–11; 26:12–18). It may even be why we are told that Paul was a maker of tents.

Missionary progress in the second half of Acts is a continued exodus cycle. Believers are forever leaving cities—often where they have been suffering—before venturing off into foreign lands, flourishing and succeeding, incorporating Gentiles in their number, and returning in triumph. More specifically we have Peter, who was going to be killed at Passover by the wicked king, waking up at nighttime, being told by the angel of the Lord to get dressed and put on his sandals, escaping captivity, and passing through a gate that opens for him "of its own accord" (Acts 12:10). This causes pandemonium among the soldiers, and soon afterward the wicked king is struck down by an angel. And in the final chapters, as Paul approaches Rome, we have yet another echo of the exodus: Paul escapes from the chains of captivity, goes on a journey for which we have an unusual level of geographical detail, and plunges into the sea, before emerging vindicated on the far side, revealing the healing power of God, and continuing toward his final destination.

The twist in the tale is that the final destination, to which the whole story of Acts has been pointing, is not Israel but Rome. This has been Paul's focus all along; he has been as committed to reaching Rome, come what may, as Israel was to getting into the Promised Land. This tells us a lot. It tells us that, for Luke, the bringing of the Gentiles into God's chosen people is no longer an interesting detail on the fringes of the exodus story, but the entire point of that story. It also tells us that, for Paul, even the dramatic events of his own lifetime have not exhausted God's redemption. He will not be satisfied until the exodus has gone global.

Review Questions

1. How is Pentecost similar and different from Sinai?
2. How is Saul of Tarsus's call like that of Moses?
3. How does the book of Acts reveal the new direction of God's mission?

Thought Questions

1. How can the story of 2 Kings 2 shed light on the relationship between Christ's ascension and Pentecost?
2. Peter presents Jesus as the "prophet like Moses" foretold in Deuteronomy 18:15–19. How is Jesus like Moses in the book of Acts?
3. In what ways is Acts 12 both a Passover story and a resurrection story?

21

Paul's Gospel

Romans–Jude

Evangelicals love summarizing the gospel. It is hardly surprising; we are *evangel*-icals, "gospel people," after all. We summarize it with illustrations: here's you, here's God, here's a chasm separating us, and here's how Jesus bridges it. We summarize it with parables, some of them biblical (the prodigal son) and some of them horribly unbiblical (but let's not go there). We identify organizing themes: the kingdom, substitution, personal relationship, wrath, heaven. Some of us use creeds. Some of us use spiritual laws: God loves me, I have sinned, Jesus died for me, I need to decide. We summarize it with songs and stories, sinners' prayers and leading questions, personal testimonies, and alphabet soup.

One summary we hardly ever use, but which appears in Paul's writings all the time—even when he is primarily talking about something else—goes something like this: We were slaves.

We were slaves to sin, death, fear, the flesh, and the Devil. But at just the right time, God rescued us. He defeated our enemy and redeemed us through the blood of his Son, taking us through the waters of baptism, uniting us to himself, giving us his Spirit to lead us and guide us, and providing us with all we need. He did all this, not so that we could do our own thing, but so that we could do his thing. And he is taking us on toward a new creation of resurrection and victory, milk and honey.

In other words: Paul's gospel is an exodus.

We see it in Galatians. We were God's children, but we were also enslaved, waiting for the time God had set. When that time came, God sent forth his Son to redeem those who were under the law, so that we might receive adoption as sons and daughters. And because we are sons and daughters, God has sent the Spirit of his Son into our hearts, crying, "Abba, Father!" (Gal. 4:6). As a result, we are no longer slaves, but children, and destined for an inheritance. So don't turn back and submit to slavery! Keep in step with God's Spirit, and you'll inherit the promises and find fruit in abundance: not just clusters of grapes, but love, joy, peace, and the rest (Gal. 4:1–6; 5:1, 16–24).

We see it in 1 Corinthians. Christ is our Passover Lamb, sacrificed to redeem us, and he calls us to be an unleavened people. Through him we have become temples where God lives by his Spirit. But bear this in mind: our fathers were all baptized into Moses in the cloud and in the sea. They all ate spiritual food (manna/bread), and they all drank spiritual drink (water/wine). Even the Rock they drank from was Jesus Christ. Yet they still blew it in the wilderness. They worshiped idols, and fell into sexual immorality, and tested God, and grumbled, and eventually God destroyed lots of them. "Now these things happened to them as an example, but they were written down for our instruction, on whom the end of the ages has come" (1 Cor. 10:11; see 3:16–17; 5:6–8; 10:1–13).

It is there in 2 Corinthians. Moses carved letters on tablets of stone; we have the Spirit written on tablets of human hearts. Moses's old covenant ministry brought condemnation and was temporary; our new covenant ministry brings glory and lasts forever. He covered his face with a veil, to ensure the divine glory could not be seen by everybody; Jesus removes the veil, to ensure that it can. For now, we host God's Spirit in a tent, as Moses did; one day, we will be given a house. So come out and separate yourselves from the land of idols (2 Cor. 3:1–18; 5:1–10; 6:14–18)!

Most emphatically, it is there in Romans. We were all enslaved to sin, bound by the law, and under the rule of death. But God redeemed us through Jesus Christ (Rom. 3:21–26). We were buried with him in baptism, with our old slave master dead in the waters behind us (6:1–14). We immediately found joy in serving our new master (6:15–23), experiencing both freedom from the law (7:1–25) and new life in the Spirit (8:1–11). For now, we continue living as children and heirs, with God's Spirit among us, rather than slipping back into slavery (8:12–17)—but we look forward to the new Land of Promise, in which not only our bodies but creation itself will be set free from slavery to corruption and liberated into the freedom that God's children were always supposed to inherit (8:18–25). With that future in mind, we wait with patience, secure in the love God has demonstrated to us in Christ (8:26–39).[1]

It is worth spelling this out for a couple of reasons. Partly, it may be reassuring to hear that we have not just been blowing smoke in this book. The echoes of the exodus that we have heard throughout Scripture were also heard by Paul, in rich surround sound, and they provide a crucial narrative context for his gospel. Debate often swirls as to which "model" or "image" of the atonement is most central to Paul—reconciliation, justification, victory, penal substitution, and so on—but when it is laid out like this, it is difficult to avoid concluding that the language of *redemption*, understood through the story of Passover and exodus, is at least as important as the others. Given that both of the sacraments echo this story as well, with the Lord's Supper a reenactment of Passover and baptism of the parting of the Red Sea, we could even say: perhaps more so.[2]

Yet Paul's exodus-shaped gospel also presents a challenge to us, which comes through clearly in all four of these epistles. God has set us free from slavery, Paul explains, not so that we might serve nobody at all—which, in the end, amounts to serving ourselves—but so that we might serve God. Time and again, in these texts and elsewhere, Paul uses the exodus story not just to remind Christians of our liberty, but also of our responsibility. "Stand firm therefore, and do not submit again to a yoke of slavery." "Flee from idolatry." "Do not be unequally yoked with unbelievers." "How can we who died to sin still live in it?" And so on (Gal. 5:1; 1 Cor. 10:14; 2 Cor. 6:14; Rom. 6:2).

Other apostles use the exodus story in a similar way: as a way of encouraging and warning Christians that they must continue in faith. Jude reminds his readers that although Jesus saved a people from Egypt—and we should note, in passing, the matter-of-fact way in which he says *Jesus* did this (Jude 5)— he afterward destroyed those who did not believe.[3] Hebrews points out that although Israel left Egypt under Moses, many of them hardened their hearts into unbelief and rebellion; if we don't want to face the same judgment they did, we need to press on in faith until we "enter into rest," even if it costs us imprisonment, ostracism, and shame (Hebrews 4). So yes, the exodus is a beautiful picture of what God has done. But it is also a challenging picture of what we are to do.

This exposes something that seems obscure in the book of Exodus, but is actually at the heart of Christian discipleship: Israel was set free from serving one master *in order that they might serve a new one*. God's purpose for the plagues and the confrontations, the water-crossings and the fire, was not that Israel might be free to wander off and do their own thing, but that they might "serve" him (Ex. 7:16; 8:1, 20; 9:1, 13; 10:3). The contrast in Exodus, in fact, is less between slavery and freedom, as we might expect, and more between slavery to Pharaoh (which, although we may not have noticed it, also characterizes the Egyptians!) and service to the Lord.[4] It is as if, within the context of the exodus story, service to nobody is not an option.

Israel cannot cope without serving someone, and neither can we. When a football team buys a new player, they do not set him free from one master so he can play the game on his own somewhere. They set him free from one master so that he can play for another; players simply cannot function without a team to serve. And human beings, as worshipers, are just the same. We are made to worship, and will find a new master even if it kills us. This is one of the tragedies of the golden calf incident: no sooner has Israel stopped serving one false god (Pharaoh) that they want to start serving another (an idol). David Foster Wallace famously put it like this:

> In the day-to-day trenches of adult life, there is actually no such thing as atheism. There is no such thing as not worshipping. Everybody worships. The only choice we get is what to worship. And an outstanding reason for choosing some sort of God or spiritual-type thing to worship—be it J. C. or Allah, be it Yahweh or the Wiccan mother-goddess or the Four Noble Truths or some infrangible set of ethical principles—is that pretty much anything else you worship will eat you alive.[5]

That's what the exodus generation found out. It's what Hebrews and Jude warned local churches about. It's what Joshua meant when he urged Israel to "choose this day whom you will serve," because he knew they would end up serving somebody, and it was just a question of whom (Josh. 24:15). Paul is even blunter in Romans 6: we are all slaves. Either we serve sin, leading to death, or we serve obedience, leading to righteousness. Those who serve Pharaoh become beasts and perish. Those who serve the Lord become priests and flourish.

Four and a half centuries ago, a group of theologians gathered in Heidelberg, Germany, to explain their Reformation theology in a question-and-answer format. The first question they asked was this: "What is my only comfort in life and in death?" They answered with one of the most beautiful paragraphs in the history of Christian theology, with Paul's exodus-shaped vision of the gospel ("paid for," "set free from tyranny") sandwiched in between two statements of the exchange of masters that we have been looking at in this chapter. What is my only hope?

> *That I am not my own*, but belong—body and soul, in life and in death—to my faithful Savior, Jesus Christ. He has fully paid for all my sins with his precious blood, and has set me free from the tyranny of the devil. He also watches over me in such a way that not a hair can fall from my head without the will of my Father in heaven; in fact, all things must work together for my salvation. *Because I belong to him*, Christ, by his Holy Spirit, assures me of eternal life and makes me wholeheartedly willing and ready from now on to live for him.[6]

Paid for, set free, watched over, assured. But not only that: owned.

Review Questions

1. How does the book of Romans present our salvation using an exodus framework?
2. How does the exodus-shaped presentation of salvation provide us with a warning and challenge?
3. What are some of the ways in which Paul presents his gospel of exodus as a deliverance *from*? What are some of the ways in which he presents it as a deliverance *for* and *to*?

Thought Questions

1. How does 1 Corinthians 10 present the relationship between the church and the children of Israel brought out from Egypt?
2. How is the Christian compared and contrasted with the figure of Moses and with the children of Israel in 2 Corinthians 3:7–18?
3. How does the theme of exodus run through the book of Hebrews? What can we learn from comparing Isaiah 63:11–14 and Hebrews 13:20–21?

22

The Exodus of Everything

Revelation

Every exodus in Scripture is incomplete, except the last one. The patriarchs leave the land and come back wealthy, but their descendants are enslaved. Moses leads the people out of Egypt, but they die in the wilderness. Joshua takes them into the Land, but the Canaanites remain. David and Solomon secure the Land and build the temple, but Israel divides. Exile is followed by return, but idolatry continues. Jesus goes into the depths and emerges victorious, but leaves when the conquest of the Land has hardly started. The church marches out in the power of the Spirit, but as the Epistles clearly show, the church is still in the wilderness, awaiting its final rest, looking to the day when "death of death, and hell's destruction, land me safe on Canaan's side."[1] Every time we think the melody is complete, there is a further complication, another discordant note. Exodus, but. Exodus, but.

Until Revelation. Finally, at the last exodus, the chord resolves. Creation itself, led by the victorious children of God, steps out of slavery into the glorious liberty it was always intended for, free at last and joyful forever. There are no more wars to fight or idols to dethrone. There is no remaining Achan or Pharaoh, no further Jericho or Ai. The commander of the Lord's army is here, the dragon has been hurled into the deep, and the wicked city has fallen. Now there is nothing but clusters of grapes and hills lined with fig trees, milk and honey, justice and joy, springs of water, and rivers of wine.

The whole book of Revelation has an exodus shape to it. It begins, like the story of Moses, with awe-inspiring visions of God (chaps. 1, 4) alongside promises of the rescue that will come at the end of the church's sufferings (2–3). This rescue comes through a slain Lamb, like the Passover lamb, who appears in response to the cries of God's people, ransoms them, and makes them kings and priests (5). The people of Israel are sealed, so that they cannot be destroyed by the judgments coming on the world (7); those "coming out of the great tribulation" (like Egypt; Rev. 7:14) include people from every tribe and nation (like Israel), and they are guided by a shepherd (like Moses) to streams of living water and to serve God in his temple (like the exodus).

The throne of God, like Mount Sinai, is accompanied by thunder, lightning, earthquakes, smoke, and trumpets (Revelation 8). Two witnesses, like Moses and Aaron, are sent by God to prophesy, and they are opposed by the evil ruler and his magic-working false prophet (11; 13). Plagues are sent from heaven, including water turning to blood, frogs, boils, heavy hailstones, locusts, and darkness (9–16).[2] As the cosmic battle builds, a dragon figure (like Pharaoh) tries to kill the male child of a woman (like Moses) and sweep her away in a river (as at the Red Sea), but she is carried away on eagle's wings into the wilderness, and the dragon is hurled down and conquered by the blood of the Lamb (12). Their victory accomplished, God's people "sing the song of Moses, the servant of God, and the song of the Lamb" (Rev. 15:3), and we see the tabernacle opened (15). Finally, as in Joshua, we have the conquest of the land: after the blasts of seven trumpets, we see the collapse of the wicked city where the prostitute lives (17–18), the defeat of the enemy by the commander of the Lord's army (19–20), and the establishment of a new land, a new city, and a new temple (21–22).

It is the perfect way for the Scriptures to conclude. This is not just because it resolves the plot, enabling us to say with complete confidence that "they all lived happily ever after." It is also because, by ending with the exodus of everything, this kind of conclusion reveals to us what type of story we have been reading all along. The Bible is a redemption story. It is a cosmic exodus, stretching from Eden to the New Jerusalem. All the exodus narratives we have seen in this book—political, geographical, spiritual, liturgical—are contained within a global one that only comes to completion at the return of Christ. So if, at times, it has seemed like we are going round in circles, making bricks without straw, trapped in slavery to sin and death for century upon painful century, and crying out for someone to help us, that is because we have been. When Adam sinned, we left our homeland, fell into captivity, and have been hoping to get back ever since.

So have the oceans. So have the forests. Paul's teaching in Romans 8 is remarkable here: it is not just human beings who are awaiting redemption, but "*creation itself* will be set free from its bondage to corruption and obtain the freedom of the glory of the children of God" (v. 21). We are looking forward to the exodus of *everything*. When we left Eden and headed into Egypt, we took the cedars and the swordfish and the puffins with us. The physical world, over which we were given dominion, suffered the consequences of exile and ruptured *shalom*. Like

151

a woman in labor, creation as a whole is crying out in anguish, straining toward the day when her labor pains will be over and the new creation will break out from inside the old.

And when our true and better Joshua returns to lead us across the Jordan, creation will come too. We will rise up from the riverbed followed by a multicolored menagerie of flora and fauna, like a latter-day Noah emerging from the depths and blinking at the brightness, to find that the waters have receded and there is no longer any sea. There is a new heaven and a new earth, not just a new Jerusalem. The labor pains were worth it. Paul was right: the weight of glory makes our light and momentary afflictions seem trivial. Tolkien was right: everything sad has become untrue.[3] Lewis was right: the dream has ended, and this is the morning.[4] Dostoevsky was right:

> In the world's finale, at the moment of eternal harmony, something so precious will come to pass that it will suffice for all hearts, for the comforting of all resentments, for the atonement of all the crimes of humanity, for all the blood that they've shed; that it will make it not only possible to forgive but to justify all that has happened.[5]

Death has been swallowed up in victory. The enemy who once harassed us and threatened us has been obliterated, and his entire army with him, and the whole world looks different. High-rises have become orchards. Children are no longer hiding indoors for fear of neighbors or potential predators, but are chasing and laughing and playing in the streets. The desert is in bloom. The mountains and the hills have broken forth into singing. The trees of the fields are clapping their hands. Death is no more, and neither is there any mourning, or crying, or pain, for the former things have passed away. Further up, and further in![6]

"He who testifies to these things says, 'Surely I am coming soon.' Amen. Come, Lord Jesus!" (Rev. 22:20).

Review Questions

1. How does the general story line of Revelation recall the exodus story?
2. How does Revelation extend the scope of Exodus?
3. What is the character of the new Promised Land?

Thought Questions

1. How might the story of Joshua, Rahab, and the defeat of Jericho shed light on the destruction of the city in Revelation and the relationship between it and the bride?
2. How does the conclusion of Revelation return us to Eden? How do exodus and Eden themes relate?
3. How is the glorious Mount Zion of Revelation like Mount Sinai? How is it different?

Coda

Living the Exodus

The task of the church can be described in all sorts of ways, but one of my favorites is this: we are called to make the echoes of the exodus louder. We have been given the responsibility and the privilege of standing in the middle of this epic story and witnessing to it. People all around us, going about their daily business, do not recognize the Pharaohs and the plagues, the manna from heaven and the chariots in the deep. Part of the task of the church is to amplify the music of redemption, so that they (and we) might hear it for what it truly is.

The most obvious way we do that is by celebrating the sacraments. Consider: Jesus gave two sacraments to his church, and they both enact the exodus. In baptism, we celebrate the burial of the old, the passing from death into life, and the drowning of our enemies in floodwaters. In the Eucharist, we remember how God ransomed us from slavery to sin and death through the blood of a Lamb, uniting us both to him and to one another. Whenever we baptize someone or share in the Lord's Supper, we are witnessing to ourselves, and to the world around us, that all of us have known slavery. All of us live in hope of a land flowing with milk and honey. And Israel's God has stepped down to liberate us from the former, and take us triumphantly into the latter.

We are saying more than that, too. In baptism we declare not only our liberation from the Pharaoh of sin, but we declare our new identity as a kingdom of priests to God. In baptism we are baptized into the promised Prophet who is greater than Moses. In baptism we are manifested as those joined to the multitude of a new people, born again through divine deliverance; we are seen as led by the pillar of the Spirit, into the new creation. In baptism, we are washed in the same waters that were divided in the second and third days of creation, brought through the waters of the flood, carried through the trial of the ford of the Jabbok, and taken up from the Red Sea. In baptism, our bodies are marked out for resurrection, for entrance into the new creation. We walk in the same path as Noah, Abraham, Isaac, Jacob, Joseph, Moses, Israel, Ruth, Hannah, Samuel, David, Solomon, Elijah and Elisha, Isaiah, Jeremiah, Ezekiel, Esther, Ezra, and Nehemiah. We walk in the path of Jesus Christ: the way of exodus.

Similar things are true of the Lord's Supper. Every time we celebrate it, we are drawn back to the Last Supper—to *that night*—and, beyond that, to all of the many exoduses and passovers that preceded it. Not for nothing did Jesus tell us, "Do this, as often as you drink it, in remembrance of me" (1 Cor. 11:25). Yet we are also drawn forward to that which we await in the future: the great marriage supper, for which the bread and wine are the entrée. "I will not drink again of the fruit of this vine until that day when I drink it new with you in my Father's kingdom" (Matt. 26:29). Or, as Paul put it, "As often as you eat this bread and drink the cup, you proclaim the Lord's death until he comes" (1 Cor. 11:26).

As we share in the sacraments, our bodies are caught up in the rhythm of redemption, echoing our past deliverance but also anticipating our future one. The music we have been listening to in this book, in other words, is not just something we *hear* but also something we *participate in* as we share the Lord's Supper and baptize one another. The music moves our souls and animates our bodies. We become part of it, and it becomes part of us. We enter into the biblical symphony because it is *ours*, not just *theirs*. As we tear the loaf and share the cup, we are Joshua and Caleb, remembering the Passover meal, but we are also tasting the grapes of Eshcol and reveling in the wine to come. As we pass through the waters of baptism, we join with Moses and Miriam on the far shore of the sea, singing both of what God has done and of what he will do, knowing that the God who held back the waters of the Red Sea will make short work of the Jordan.

This symbolic performance of the exodus, transposed into a Christian key, is then filled out and amplified by the rest of our weekly worship. We sing songs of redemption and rescue. We pray to the God who hears our cries for deliverance and thank him for his mighty acts. We read and study the story of God's people. We bring financial offerings for God's house. We are sent out, in the power of the Spirit, in the knowledge that the journey is not yet over.

We live daily life in the wilderness. We rely on God's provision for our water, our clothing, and our daily bread. We follow the cloud of God's presence wherever it goes. We live not by bread alone but by every word that comes from the mouth of God (Matt. 4:4). We renounce the worship of idols and all that goes with it: sexual immorality, injustice, greed, drunkenness, rebellion, grumbling, and unbelief. We preach the gospel of redemption to those around us. When we face opposition, whether from enemies of God's people (Amalek), religious charlatans (Balaam), temptations to sin (Moab), or our own flesh, we stand firm. When we encounter those who do not know the Lord, we invite them as Moses invited Hobab: "Come with us, and we will do good to you, for the Lord has promised good to Israel" (Num. 10:29).

We also live as those who have recently been released from centuries of oppression: that is, with a preferential option for the poor, and a commitment to champion the cause of those who have been abused, bullied, captured, disenfranchised, enslaved, forgotten, ghettoized, hated, ignored, judged, killed, lynched, marginalized, and so on throughout the alphabet. Exodus people know what it is to be ground into the dust by those with power. So whenever we see it happening to others—racial minorities, slaves, trafficked women, the poor, unborn children, refugees, the homeless, those with disabilities, sojourners, orphans, widows—we act. We march. We speak. We pray. We invite. We give. We use our power to serve the interests of those without it, because the exodus was never just for us. Free people free people.

And of course, we tell this story. We tell it to our children, and we write it on our doorposts. The God of the exodus is the unchanging "I am"; he was there for us in Goshen and Ararat and Babylon and Jerusalem, and he will always be there for us in the future. He brings us out and he brings us in, and when we come back, we always find ourselves with more than we started with. One day the Jordan will divide, and the trumpets will sound, and worldly powers will collapse, and the vines will stretch as far as the eye can see. But in the meantime, as we look forward to that and look back to our deliverance from Egypt, we have a song to sing:

> I will sing to the Lord, for he has triumphed gloriously;
>   the horse and his rider he has thrown into the sea.
> The Lord is my strength and my song,
>   and he has become my salvation;
> this is my God, and I will praise him,
>   my father's God, and I will exalt him. (Ex 15:1–2)

Review Questions

1. How does baptism proclaim exodus? How does baptism bring us into the music of the story of redemption?
2. How does the Lord's Supper both draw us back and propel us forward?
3. How does exodus inform mission?

Thought Questions

1. How do themes of exodus play out on different interlocking levels of our lives: as individuals, churches, societies, peoples, etc.?
2. How does being caught up in the music of exodus change the way that we read and hear Scripture?
3. How can we make our lives more "musical," more charged with the tensions and the resolutions of the great work of God's deliverance?

Notes

Prelude: Echoes of the Exodus

1. Obviously this could easily descend into silliness: "I went to the store to buy milk" could become an exodus story in which I leave the house of slavery, cross the Red Sea of my street, press on to receive my inheritance (a land flowing with milk?), and return to my homeland with more than I started with. Ultimately it is impossible to draw a clear line between this absurdity and what follows in this book, so the proof of the pudding will have to be in the eating.

2. The historian Eric Hobsbawm, in his four-volume history of the modern world from 1789 to 1991, identifies the most drastic transformation of all as "the disintegration of the old patterns of social relationships and with it, incidentally, the snapping of the links between generations, that is to say, between past and present" (*The Age of Extremes: The Short Twentieth Century, 1914–1991* [London: Abacus, 1994], 15).

3. This is not to make any comment about whether followers of Jesus today are ever supposed to use violence or take up arms—as it happens, the authors of this volume disagree with each other on those points—but it should at least be clear that Joshua was supposed to.

4. Of all the texts in the Gospels, Luke 17:22–37, with its mentions of cataclysmic floods, fire and sulphur, and pillars of salt, is particularly difficult to square with the view that Jesus was correcting the Old Testament on this point. Marcionism is the idea that the God revealed in Jesus is fundamentally different from the God of the Old Testament.

5. A compelling recent work that integrates all kinds of different atonement motifs, and shows how they coexist in Scripture, is Fleming Rutledge, *The Crucifixion: Understanding the Death of Jesus Christ* (Grand Rapids, MI: Eerdmans, 2015).

6. A more esoteric example: the big debate in Pauline scholarship at present is between those who think Paul's gospel emphasizes Christ as the fulfillment of Israel's long story and those who think it emphasizes Christ as a dramatically new thing that God has done in the world. The exodus story provides a wonderful paradigm for seeing how it is both: God acts—dramatically and in a completely unprecedented way—to liberate Israel from slavery, in fulfillment of his centuries-old promise to Abraham. The exodus is thus both "apocalyptic" and "covenantal," both continuous and discontinuous with what has gone before; so too is the work of Jesus. Or, as Tom Wright is fond of putting it, "God has acted shockingly, surprisingly, startlingly, as he always said he would," Andrew Wilson, "Tom Wright Skewers the New Marcionism," *Think* (blog), May 29, 2013, http://thinktheology.co.uk/blog/article/tom_wright_skewers_the_new_marcionism/.

Chapter 2: The First Supper

1. Charles Taylor, *A Secular Age* (London: The Belknap Press of Harvard University Press, 2007), 58.

Chapter 4: The Battle of the Gods

1. D. A. Carson, *Scandalous: The Cross and Resurrection of Jesus* (Wheaton, IL: Crossway, 2010), 100–101.

Chapter 5: True Freedom

1. From the foreword of Neil Postman, *Amusing Ourselves to Death: Public Discourse in the Age of Show Business* (New York: Penguin, 1986).

Chapter 6: Journey's End

1. See, for example, Joshua Ryan Butler, *The Skeletons in God's Closet: The Mercy of Hell, the Surprise of Judgment, the Hope of Holy War* (Nashville: Thomas Nelson, 2014), 207–302.

Chapter 8: Russian Dolls

1. Custom dictated that a woman's brother was responsible for vetting potential suitors (e.g., Gen. 24:29–31, 50–51, 60; 34), so on hearing that Abram was Sarai's brother—which, as we later discover, was sort of true—Pharaoh should have consulted him, rather than simply taking his sister/wife. It also appears that husbands might easily have been killed by more powerful men, eager to seize their wives. Thus Abram's deception was intended to protect both his wife and his family by buying time as an honorable brother rather than being immediately killed as an unwanted husband—and not merely to save his own skin.

Chapter 10: Wrestling with God

1. C. S. Lewis, *The Horse and His Boy* (Glasgow: Fontana Lions, 1980), 139.

Chapter 11: Wings of Refuge

1. Thanks to Peter Leithart for this point. See his articles: "When Gentile Meets Jew: A Christian Reading of Ruth and the Hebrew Scriptures," *Touchstone Magazine*, May, 2009, http://www.touchstonemag.com /archives/article.php?id=22-04-020-f and "The Structures of Ruth," *Biblical Horizons Newsletter* 45, January 1993, http://www.biblical horizons.com/biblical-horizons/no-45-the-structures-of-ruth/.

Chapter 14: The End of the Exodus?

1. See Amos Frisch's stimulating treatment of 1 Kings 1–14 in "The Exodus Motif in 1 Kings 1–14," *Journal for the Study of the Old Testament* 87 (2000), 3–21.

2. Peter Leithart, *1 & 2 Kings*, SCM Theological Commentary on the Bible (Grand Rapids, MI: Brazos Press, 2006), 56–58.

Chapter 15: Elijah and Elisha

1. Compare 1 Kings 18:41 with Exodus 24:9–11.

Chapter 16: The Outstretched Arm

1. See Nevada Levi DeLapp, "Ezekiel as Moses—Israel as Pharaoh: Reverberations of the Exodus Narrative in Ezekiel," in R. Michael Fox, ed., *Reverberations of the Exodus in Scripture* (Eugene, OR: Pickwick Publications, 2014), 51–73, for a more detailed exploration of these themes.

Chapter 17: Purim and Purity

1. It is somewhat confusing that these two returns take place ninety years apart, even though Ezra and Nehemiah were contemporaries. The reason for this is that the first six chapters of Ezra are set in the past, at the time of Cyrus's decree (538 BC), whereas the last four and the whole of Nehemiah are set in the 450s and 440s BC.

2. The parallels between Ezra-Nehemiah and Exodus-Numbers here can also help us make sense of one of the most troubling passages in the Old Testament, namely the ban on intermarriage and the driving out of foreign wives and their children (Ezra 9–10; cf. Nehemiah 13). Countless readers have been disturbed by what looks like an outright ban on interracial relationships and the practice of splitting up families accordingly. But three clues in the context reveal that this is a specific measure to cope with a specific problem. (1) We can identify echoes of the exodus. Intermarriage with foreign women in this context recalls

Israel's immorality with Moab just before they entered the land, for which twenty-four thousand Israelites died in a plague of divine judgment (Numbers 25; cf. 1 Corinthians 10). (2) Nehemiah explains that the Israelites had only just sealed a covenant (Nehemiah 10), yet then proceeded to violate every one of its stipulations (Nehemiah 13): no intermarriage, observing the Sabbath, and supporting the temple and its workers (10:30–39). This line-by-line breaking of the covenant is reminiscent of the worship of the golden calf at Sinai. (3) The list of foreign nations in Ezra 9:1 is striking in itself, because it echoes the list of nations Israel was told to drive out of Canaan. Ezra-Nehemiah is presenting the return as a kind of reconquest of Canaan—which makes faithfulness to the covenant, and refusing to compromise with foreign gods, all the more important.

Chapter 18: The Crescendo

1. Like Israel in Genesis and Exodus, Jesus went down into Egypt for his own safety and then came out again, marking him out as loved by God (Hosea 11). Like Israel in the exile to Babylon, Jesus's departure from the land was accompanied by weeping and tragedy in the area around Jerusalem, but was a necessary step toward the inauguration of the new covenant (Jeremiah 31).
2. See, for example, Richard Hays, *Echoes of Scripture in the Gospels* (Waco: Baylor, 2016), 20–24.
3. The phrase in Matthew 9:36 is taken directly from Numbers 27:17.
4. Both stories include a sword and the phrase "I have come," which may be significant; see Simon Gathercole, *The Preexistent Son: Recovering the Christologies of Matthew, Mark, and Luke* (Grand Rapids, MI: Eerdmans, 2006), 164.

Chapter 19: The Exodus of Jesus

1. Alastair Roberts, "Transfigured Hermeneutics—Transfiguration and Exodus," *reformation 21*, December 18, 2015, http://www.reformation 21.org/blog/2015/12/transfigured-hermeneutics-tran.php/.
2. The fact that Judas betrays Jesus with a kiss also reminds us of Joab (2 Sam. 20:9).

Chapter 21: Paul's Gospel

1. On the exodus theme in Paul, see the various works of N. T. Wright, especially *Paul and the Faithfulness of God* (London: SPCK, 2013), 774–1042, and *The Day the Revolution Began* (London: SPCK, 2016), 227–351.
2. Having said that, Paul's dominant language for the effect of the gospel is that we are now "in Christ," and so it is probably this theme—which

of course is intimately connected with Christ's victory, substitutionary death, redemption, ministry of reconciliation, and so on—that stands at the center.

3. Some versions retain "the Lord" in Jude 5, but the weight of manuscript evidence suggests the original text had "Jesus."

4. The Egyptians are repeatedly described as "slaves" or "servants" of Pharaoh. See Exodus 7:10, 20; 8:3, 4, 9, 11, 21, 29, 31; 9:14, 20, 30, 34; 10:1, 6, 7; 11:3, 8; 12:30; 14:5.

5. David Foster Wallace, *This Is Water: Some Thoughts, Delivered on a Significant Occasion, on Living a Compassionate Life* (New York: Little, Brown & Company, 2009).

6. The Heidelberg Catechism, Lord's Day 1. Emphasis mine.

Chapter 22: The Exodus of Everything

1. William Williams, "Guide Me, O Thou Great Jehovah," 1745.

2. We could go further: on the two occasions that Revelation counts the plagues, there are three (9:18) followed by seven (15:1), making a total of ten, which also corresponds to the exodus story. On this whole chapter, including this theme, see Peter Leithart, *Revelation*, 2 vols. (London: T&T Clark, 2017).

3. J. R. R. Tolkien, *The Lord of the Rings* (London: HarperCollins, 2005), 951.

4. C. S. Lewis, *The Last Battle* (New York: Collier, 1970), 183.

5. Fyodor Dostoevsky, *The Brothers Karamazov* (London: Wordsworth, 2007), 257.

6. Lewis, *The Last Battle*, 167.

General Index

1812 Overture, 109
1984, 15, 51

Aaron, 49, 72, 101–2, 105–6, 125, 132–33, 150
Abel, 61
Abigail, 88
Abihu (son of Aaron), 102, 132
Abijah (son of Jeroboam), 102
Abimelech, 72, 90
Abishai, 134
Abraham
    exodus journeys of, 65–69, 129, 156
    faith of, 66, 68, 70–71
    father of many nations, 70, 74, 137
    generational pattern of exodus, 65, 68, 70–74, 156
    parallels to, 66–68, 70–71, 125
Abrahamic covenant, 68, 137, 161n6 (chap. 1)
Abram. *See* Abraham
Absalom, 96, 98, 134
Achan, 56–57, 96, 107, 139, 150
Adam, 35–36, 49, 61, 63–64, 101, 103, 151
adoption, 16, 36, 143
Ahab, 105–8, 136
Ahaziah, 105
Ahithophel, 134
Allah, 146
Amalekites, 95, 98, 117, 139, 157
Amnon, 96
Ananias and Sapphira, 57, 139
angel of the Lord
    encounters with, 26, 107, 126, 135
    saving work of, 30, 54–56, 71–74, 93, 113, 127, 134, 139, 140
    wrestling with Jacob, 76–79

Anna, 126
"Anthem for Doomed Youth," 109
Aphek, 89, 91
ark
    of the Lord, 55, 85, 89–92, 96–97
    of Moses, 36, 62–64, 114
    of Noah, 36, 44, 62–64, 127
Artaxerxes, 119
Ashdod, 90–91
Asherah, 105–6
Aslan, 78
Assyria, 104, 112–13
atheism, 146
atonement, 16, 144, 160n5, 163–64n2 (chap. 21)

Baal, 105–6
Babel, Tower of, 65–66, 69, 137–38
Babylon, 104, 111–13, 158, 163n1 (chap. 18)
Balaam, 157
Balak, 110
baptism
    of Jesus, 44, 127, 130, 156
    into Moses, 39, 143
    parallel to creation, 44, 63–64, 156
    parallel to Noah's ark, 44, 63–64, 156
    parallel to water crossings, 44, 77, 145, 155–59
Barabbas, 134
Bathsheba, 96
Beethoven, Ludwig van, 24
Berg, Peter, 23
Boaz, 83–87
Brave New World, 15, 51

Cain, 61, 133
Caleb, 139, 157
Canaan, 53–54, 66–67, 70, 75–77, 149
Canaanites, 56, 67, 105–7, 127, 139, 149
church, the, 14, 138, 142, 148–50, 155, 157
circumcision, 38–39, 44, 50, 54–55, 72
Collins, Suzanne, 51
covenant
    Abrahamic covenant, 57, 68, 137, 161n6
      (chap. 1)
    Davidic covenant, 96
    Mosaic covenant, 30, 49, 119, 144
    new covenant, 29–30, 115, 137–38,
      143–44
creation, 25, 44, 62–64, 115, 151–52
Cyrus, 117, 119

Dagon, 90–91
Daniel, 111, 117
David, 26, 93–99, 134, 149, 156
Davidic covenant, 96
Day of Atonement, 25
deliverance
    marked by baptism, 156–57
    marked by the Lord's Supper, 29, 156–57
    marked by Passover, 29–31
    of Israel, 51–52, 76, 78, 117–19
    of Jesus, 107, 135, 147
    of Lot, 74
    of Moses, 39–40
    of Ruth, 85
disciples of Jesus, 128, 131–32
discipleship, Christian, 13, 47, 145
Dostoyevsky, Fyodor, 152
dragon figures, 36, 90, 94, 101, 112, 150.
    See also serpent figures

Ebenezer, 91
Eden, 35–36, 49, 61, 72, 100–101, 151, 153
Edomites, 95, 119
Egypt, 16, 28–30, 35, 44–45, 48, 66–67, 57,
    78–79, 89, 149
Eli, 88–89
Elijah, 55, 104–8, 127, 129, 131–32, 136,
    140, 156
Elimelech, 84
Elisha, 55, 105–8, 127, 136, 156
Elisheba, 125
Elizabeth, 88, 125
Enoch, 62
Ephraim, 110

Esau, 75, 77
Esther, 88, 116–20, 156
Eucharist, 30, 155. *See also* Lord's Supper
Euphrates River, 76–77
evangelicals, 14, 142
Eve, 49, 100
exile
    compared to exodus, 61, 75
    of God, 89–92
    of Israel, 29, 61, 104, 110–11, 120, 149,
      163n1 (chap. 18)
exodus
    of Abraham, 65–69, 129, 156
    of Abraham's family, 68, 70–74
    of David, 93–98, 156
    of Elijah, 104–8, 136, 156
    of Elisha, 105–8, 156
    of Esther, 116–20, 156
    of Ezekiel, 111–12, 156
    of Ezra, 156
    of God, 89–92
    of Hagar, 70–71, 74
    of Hannah, 88–92, 156
    of Isaac, 70–72, 156
    of Isaiah, 112–15, 156
    of Ishmael, 70–71, 74
    of Israel, 156; end of, 99–103; from
      Babylon, 113; from Egypt, 16, 35,
      44, 57; parallels to, 62–63, 138, 153;
      remembered with Passover, 28–30; two
      halves of, 48, 66
    of Jacob, 75, 77, 156
    of Jeremiah, 29, 111, 126, 156
    of Jesus, 125–30, 131–36, 156
    of Joseph, 78, 156
    of Joshua, 53–58, 107
    of Lot, 72–74
    of Moses, 35–46, 110, 114, 156
    of Naomi, 83–87
    of Nehemiah, 156
    of Noah, 44, 61–64, 133, 156
    of Rebekah, 70–72
    of Ruth, 83–87, 156
    of Samuel, 89–92, 156
    of Solomon, 156
exodus stories
    as a battle of the gods, 41–46, 56, 88,
      90–92, 94, 105–6, 150
    centrality to Scripture, 13, 17, 27
    fulfilled in Christ, 16, 26, 30–31, 43, 92,
      136, 149, 161n6 (chap. 1)

role of the Holy Spirit in, 115, 135, 137
role of women in, 35–36, 54, 70–71, 77,
 88–89, 135
as source of hope, 115, 127
themes in: adoption, 16, 36, 143;
 baptism, 16, 44, 63–64, 127, 143,
 156–59; birth, 40, 44, 62, 76, 89,
 126, 129; blood sacrifice, 16, 41, 147;
 faith, 16, 39, 43, 50, 68, 70, 106,
 145; firstborn sons, 38, 42–44, 71,
 129, 134; inheritance, 41, 54, 57, 66,
 77–78, 95, 120, 138, 143; kingdom,
 16, 27, 151; liberation, 16, 51–52 (*see
 also* freedom); oppression, 16, 41, 88,
 158; Passover, 16, 43, 143; plagues,
 41–42, 150, 155; priesthood, 16,
 36, 62, 73, 102, 138, 147, 150, 156;
 redemption, 16, 41, 86, 88, 119, 151,
 156–57; substitution, 16, 89, 95, 134,
 142, 144; union with God, 16, 147,
 163–64n2 (chap. 21); victory, 16, 25,
 41, 45, 50, 55, 57, 94, 109, 143, 144,
 150–52; wilderness, 16, 41 (*see also*
 wilderness, the)
unfinished, 31, 107, 149
Ezekiel, 111–12, 115, 156, 162n1 (chap. 16)
Ezra, 120–21, 156

faith
 of Abraham, 66, 68, 70–71
 of Elijah, 106
 of Gentiles, 56, 133
 of Israel, 66
 of Moses, 39
 obedience, 43, 48–49, 66, 145–47
fall stories, 35–36, 49–50, 56–57, 61, 63,
 70–71, 101, 127, 150
Feast of Tabernacles, 119
Four Noble Truths, 146
freedom
 for creation, 150
 in Jesus, 135, 145
 from oppression, 15–16, 88, 146, 158
 for service, 48
 from sin, 14–15, 51–52, 144–47
 true freedom, 15–16, 51–52, 143–47, 158

Gehazi, 107
genocide, 56, 118
Gentiles, 44, 84, 86–87, 133–34, 140–41
Gershom, 37

Gideon, 85
God
 as Composer, 21, 24, 26
 exodus of, 89–92
 faithfulness of, 44, 48, 57, 96
 glory of, 140, 152
 grace of, 73–74
 hope in, 110, 147
 judgment of, 56, 111, 139, 145
 mercy of, 73–74, 138
 names of: Abba, Father, 143; divine name
  (tetragrammaton), 38; God Almighty,
  38; God of the exodus, 17, 86, 102,
  110, 113, 114, 158; God Heals You,
  48; God-Is-My-Banner, 38, 48; God-
  Will-Provide, 38; I AM, 38, 48, 129,
  134, 158; Immanuel, 38; Rock, 38;
  Yahweh, 48, 146
 sovereignty of, 39, 73, 129
 strength of, 45, 85, 109–15, 158
 trust in, 39, 62, 66, 68, 127
 wings of, 85–86, 150
golden calf, 16, 49–52, 56, 102, 119, 138,
 146, 162–63n2 (chap. 17)
Goliath, 94–95, 98
Goshen, 117, 158
gospel
 exodus themes in, 13, 17, 52, 68, 73,
  128–29, 135, 142–45
 of Paul, 142–48, 163–64n2 (chap. 21)
 results of, 86, 135, 137, 157
 shrinking of, 16
 summaries of, 68, 142
Gospels
 exodus themes in, 27, 129–30, 131,
  135–36
 variances in, 21, 31, 126, 134–35
Great Commission, 128

Hagar, 70–71, 74
Ham, 65
Haman, 117–18
Hamlet, 13
Hannah, 88–92, 126, 156
Haran, 66–67, 75
Heidelberg Catechism, 47, 147
Henry V, 109
Herod, 118, 131–32
Heston, Charlton, 110
Hitler, Adolf, 118
Hobab, 157

General Index

Holocaust, 29
Holy Spirit, 112, 127, 135, 137–38, 156
Hophni, 88–89
Hunger Games, The, 15, 51
Huxley, Aldous, 51

Ichabod, 89
idolatry, 51, 57, 105, 119, 139, 144–146,
149, 157
Isaac, 70–75, 77, 84, 156
Isaiah, 112–15, 148, 156
Ishmael, 70–71, 74
Israel
exile of, 29, 61, 104, 110–11, 120, 149,
163n1 (chap. 18)
exodus of (*see* exodus, of Israel)
fall story of, 49–50, 57, 101
parallels to, 49, 62–64, 67, 95, 101, 111,
126–27, 132, 134, 138, 148–50

Jabbok River, 44, 77, 156
Jacob, 75, 77, 79, 84, 98, 156
Jehoram, 105
Jehu, 107
Jeremiah, 29, 111, 126, 156
Jericho, 54–56, 77, 91, 96, 99, 105–7, 128,
150, 153
Jeroboam, 101–3
Jerusalem, 27, 96–98, 119, 131, 134, 137,
151–52, 158
Jesus
ascension of, 135, 137
baptism of, 44, 127, 130, 156
cross of, 16, 115, 137–38
death of, 30–31, 43, 79, 92, 155–56
exodus of, 114, 125–30, 131–36, 156
incarnation of, 125–27
miracles of, 107–8
names and descriptions of: angel of the
Lord, 30; arm of the Lord, 114; Bread
of Life, 31, 129; bronze serpent in the
wilderness, 129; chosen One, 127,
132; firstborn Son, 30, 129, 134; God
of the burning bush, 134; "I AM,"
129, 134; light of the world, 129;
living water, 44, 129; Lamb of God
/ Passover Lamb, 30, 129, 134, 143,
155; Lion of Judah, 103; Lord of /
provider of wine, 30, 129; the Lord
Saves, 55, 107; Man of Sorrows, 114;
mediator, 129; Messiah, 138; Prophet,

156; prophet from Judah, 102, 129;
prophet from Judea, 103; Rock, 143;
Shepherd, 30, 129; tabernacle, 129;
Word of the Lord, 139; Yeshua, 107
parallel to Abraham, 67–68
parallel to Boaz, 85–86
parallel to David, 97, 134
parallel to Elijah, 136
parallel to Elisha, 55, 107–8, 127, 136
parallel to Esther, 118–19
parallel to Ezekiel, 130
parallel to Israel, 67, 126–27, 134
parallel to Jacob, 79
parallel to John the Baptist, 126–27, 130
parallel to Josiah, 102
parallel to Joseph, 79
parallel to Joshua, 55–58, 96, 102,
107–8, 120, 126–27, 135, 152, 160n3
parallel to Moses, 30, 97, 102, 114,
126–28, 132–35, 141, 150, 156
parallel to prophet (unnamed) from
Judah, 102–3
parallel to Samson, 91–92
victory of, 25, 30, 149
Jethro, 48, 50, 77
Jezebel, 105
Jochebed, 36
Joel, 110
John the Baptist, 55, 107, 126–27, 130, 132
Jonah, 110
Jordan River, 44, 53–56, 77, 91, 96, 99,
106–7, 127, 152, 157–58
Joseph, 76–79, 111, 117, 125, 156
Joseph (earthly father of Jesus), 125
Joshua
commission of, 128
crossing the Jordan River, 44, 53–54,
91, 99
exodus of, 53–58, 107
parallel to Abraham, 66–67
parallel to the church, 157
parallel to David, 96, 149
parallel to Elisha, 55, 105–8, 127
parallel to Jesus, 55–58, 96, 102, 107–8,
120, 126–27, 135, 152, 160n3
parallel to Moses, 54–57, 108, 135, 141,
149
parallel to Paul, 146
parallel to Peter, 57, 139
parallel to Samuel, 91
parallel to Solomon, 101

Josiah, 102–4
joy, 17, 47–48, 86, 95, 113
Judas, 134, 163n2 (chap. 19)

King Lune, 78
kingdom of God, 28–31, 44, 98, 129, 135, 156
kingdom of Israel, 96, 101, 104–5, 110
Kingdom, The (2007 movie), 23

Laban, 75–77, 79
Lamech, 61–62
Laurents, Arthur, 13
law, 49, 63, 94, 97, 111, 117, 120, 132,
    138, 143–44
Leah, 77
Leithart, Peter, 11, 162n1 (chap. 11)
Levites, 138
Lewis, C. S.
    The Horse and His Boy, 78
    The Last Battle, 152
liberty. *See* freedom
Lion King, The, 13
Lord's Day, 25
Lord's Supper, 28–31, 143–45, 155–57
Lot, 72–74

manna, 95, 143–45, 155–57
Marcionism, 15, 160n4, 161n6
Mary, 88–89, 125–26, 135
matzot, 29
Melchizedek, 69
Mephibosheth, 96
Micah, 110
Miriam, 36, 110, 117, 125–26, 135, 157
Moab, 157
Mordecai, 117–18
Mosaic covenant, 30, 49, 119, 144
Moses
    ark of, 36, 62–64, 114
    deliverance of, 38–40
    exodus journeys of, 35–49, 107, 110,
        114, 156
    as mediator, 49–50, 55, 129
    meeting God at burning bush, 37–38, 129
    meeting God on Mount Sinai, 37–38, 40
    on Mount of Transfiguration, 131–32
    parallel to Adam, 49, 101
    parallel to David, 37, 93–97, 134, 149
    parallel to Elijah, 55, 105, 107, 129, 140
    parallel to Ezekiel, 111, 115, 162n1
        (chap. 16)

parallel to Hagar, 71
parallel to Israel, 100
parallel to Jeroboam, 102
parallel to Jesus, 30, 97, 102, 114,
    126–28, 132–35, 141, 150, 156
parallel to John the Baptist, 55, 107,
    127, 132
parallel to Joseph, 76–79
parallel to Joshua, 54–57, 108, 135, 141,
    149
parallel to Josiah, 102
parallel to Noah, 36, 62–63
parallel to prophet (unnamed) from
    Judah, 102–3
parallel to witnesses at Sodom, 72
parallel to witnesses at tribulation, 150
Mount Ararat, 63, 158
Mount Carmel, 105–6
Mount Horeb, 37–38, 40, 48, 106, 108. *See
    also* Mount Sinai
Mount of Olives, 97, 134, 137
Mount Sinai, 37–38, 40, 48, 52, 63, 106,
    131–32, 150, 153
Mount of Transfiguration, 131–32
Mount Zion, 153
musical analogy
    and baptism, 63
    and the Christian life, 157
    and exodus, 53, 56, 58, 125, 128–29, 159
    and Passover, 25, 28–31, 38
    in Scripture, 21–27, 58, 63, 120, 125,
        130, 159

Naaman, 107
Naboth, 105, 108
Nadab (son of Aaron), 102, 132
Nadab (son of Jeroboam), 102
Naomi, 83–87
nativity. *See* Jesus, incarnation of
Nehemiah, 120, 156
neo-Marcionism. *See* Marcionism
Nile River, 42, 106
Nimrod, 65
Nineveh, 110
Noah, 36, 44, 61–64, 127, 156

"Ode to Joy," 24
Old Testament, 14, 21, 50, 97, 105, 160n4
oppression, 16, 29, 41, 88, 119, 158
Orwell, George, 51
Owen, Wilfred, 109

General Index

Passover
  liturgy of, 29–30, 43, 151
  musical analogy and, 25, 28–31, 38
  parallel to the Lord's Supper, 28–31, 143–45
  as prelude to Christ, 30–31, 43–44, 118, 143
  types of Passover stories, 39, 55–56, 111, 118, 141, 143
Paul, 140–47
Pentecost, 25, 137–38, 141
Peter, 57, 132, 134, 139–40
Pharaoh
  parallels to, 76–77, 79, 90, 95–96, 98, 103, 105–8, 112, 117–19, 131–32, 140
  as serpent figure, 36, 94, 118, 150
Pharisees, 127, 139
Philip, 140
Philistines, 89–92
Phinehas, 88–89, 120
plagues, 38, 42–43, 56, 67, 71, 90, 105–6, 129, 134, 150
Postman, Neil, 51, 161n1 (chap. 5)
prayer, 17, 73, 88–89, 92, 97, 112, 118–19, 139, 142
Prince of Egypt, The (1998 movie), 35, 135
Promised Land, the, 26, 51, 135, 141, 144
prophet, unnamed from Judah, 102–3

Queen of Sheba, 101

Rachel, 76–77, 88
racial reconciliation, 15–16
Rahab, 55–56, 107, 128, 153
Rebekah, 70–72, 75, 88
Red Sea
  crossing of, 94, 99, 111
  parallel to baptism, 44, 145, 155–59
  parallels to other water crossings, 36, 39, 44, 53–56, 62–63, 77, 150, 157
redemption
  of the church, 14–15, 86, 114, 144, 148, 156–57
  of Israel, 41, 43, 45, 86, 88, 110, 113–14
  in Ruth, 83–87
  from slavery, 16, 41, 43, 143–46, 157
  from sin, 14, 41, 51–52, 86, 88, 113–14, 144–47, 156 (*see also* freedom, from sin)

Reformation, Protestant, 147
Rehoboam, 101–2, 104
remembrance, 29–31, 43, 109–10, 156
rest, for God's people, 26, 61–64, 145
resurrection, 25, 27, 31, 118–19, 133–36, 141, 146, 156
"Ride of the Valkyries," 114
Romeo and Juliet, 13
Ruth, 83–87, 156, 162n1 (chap. 11)

Samson, 91–92
Samuel, 89–92, 156
Sarah, 66, 88, 70–73
Sarai. *See* Sarah
Saul (apostle). *See* Paul
Saul (King of Israel), 95, 98
Scripture
  continuity of God in, 14–15, 161n6
  difficulty in reading, 21, 50, 97, 105
  historical reading of, 84, 86–87, 162n1 (chap. 11)
  metaphorical approach to, 21, 23, 27, 160n1
  musical reading of, 21–27, 58, 63, 120, 125, 130, 159 (*see also* musical analogy)
  themes in, 13–14, 26–27, 41, 53, 55, 63, 126, 142
  typology of, 26–27
  unity of, 14, 17
  violence in, 15, 56–57, 160n3
Sennacherib, 112
serpent figures, 36, 76, 90, 94–95, 101, 117–18. *See also* dragon figures
sexual ethics, 15–16
sexual immorality, 50–51, 119–20, 139, 143, 157
Shakespeare, William
  Hamlet, 13
  Henry V, 109
  Romeo and Juliet, 13
Shem, 65
Simeon, 126
sin, forgiveness of, 29, 110, 120, 138, 152
slavery
  redemption from, 14, 51–52, 144–47, 151, 156, 158 (*see also* freedom, from sin)
  to sin, 51, 113, 143–47
  universal nature of, 146–47
Soderbergh, Steven, 23

Sodom and Gomorrah, 72
Solomon, 101, 103, 149, 156
songs
  of the church, 157–58
  of David, 93, 95
  of Hannah, 88
  of the Lamb, 151
  of Mary, 126, 135
  of Moses, 85, 95, 151, 158
  of Miriam, 125, 135
"Star-Spangled Banner, The," 109
Stephen, 140

tabernacle, the, 49, 52, 100
Tchaikovsky, Pyotr Ilyich, 109
temple, the, 100, 103–4, 151
Terah, 66
Tolkien, J. R. R., 152
Tower of Babel, 65–66, 69, 137–38
Traffic (2000 movie), 23
typology of Scripture, 26–27

Wagner, Richard, 114
Wallace, David Foster, 146
water
  baptism and, 44, 63–64, 143, 157–59
  as boundary marker, 44–45, 54
  as judgment, 62–63, 94, 155
  as symbol of salvation, 39, 44, 62–64, 100
West Side Story, 13

wilderness, the
  the church in, 16, 149–50
  idolatry in, 16, 51
  Israel in, 48, 50–54, 102, 113, 133, 143, 149
  Jesus in, 127–29, 132
  as theme in exodus stories, 16, 37, 41, 66, 70–71, 78, 95–96, 107
women
  barrenness of, 66, 72–73, 88, 114
  courage of, 36, 54–55, 88, 95, 116, 125–26
  prayers of, 88–89, 118
  role in exodus stories, 35–36, 54–55, 70–71, 77, 88–89, 95, 125–26, 135
  songs of, 114, 126, 135
worship
  in the church, 14, 157
  false worship, 49, 101–2, 105–6, 133, 138–39, 143
  fueled by exodus themes, 17
  of God, 38, 47, 67, 94, 110–11, 116–17
  at the temple, 53, 97–100, 119
  true worship, 49, 53, 67, 96, 106, 111
  universality of, 146

Xerxes, 117

Zacharias, 126
Zechariah, 110–11
Zipporah, 37, 39

Scripture Index

Genesis
book of 21, 27, 35, 59,
          163n1 (chap. 18)
3 103
3–6 61
4:26 62
5:22 62
6–9 61
6:8–9 62
7:16 63
8:1 63
9 63
10–15 65
12:1–3 66
12:5 67
12:8 67
12:10–20 . . . 67, 69, 74
12:19 67
13–14 69
13:10 72
14:14 67
14:18–20 . . . 69
15 . . . . 68, 69
15:7 68
16 . . . . 70, 74
16–26 70
18 72
18:3–5 72
18:25 74
19:1 73
19:3 72
19:4–11 72
19:12–14 . . . 72
19:15–17 . . . 72
19:16 . . . . . . 73, 74
19:23–25 . . . 72

19:26 72
19:30–38 . . . 73
20 . . . . 67, 71
20:1–18 74
20:18 72
21 71
21:9–21 71
22:1–19 71
24:29–31 . . . 161n1 (chap. 8)
24:50–51 . . . 161n1 (chap. 8)
24:60 . . . . . . 161n1 (chap. 8)
25:20–34 . . . 79
26 71
26:1–11 74
26:16 71
26:22 72
27–50 75
29:1–30:24 . . 76
30:25 76
30:25–43 . . . 76
30:36 76
31:1–21 76
31:25–35 . . . 77
32:22–32 . . . 77
32:28 77
32:30 78
33:1–20 77
34 . . . . 161n1 (chap. 8)
37–45 78
40:20–22 . . . 132

Exodus
book of 49, 97, 117,
          120, 140, 145,
          146, 153, 163n1
          (chap. 18)

1 66
1–2 . . . . 61, 76, 101
1–3 35
1–19 97
2 36
2:22 37
3 38
3:1–6 140
3:12 48
4–15 41
4:1–9 41
4:24–26 38
6:23 125
7:10 . . . . 164n4 (chap. 21)
7:16 146
7:20 . . . . 164n4 (chap. 21)
8:1 146
8:3 . . . . 164n4 (chap. 21)
8:4 . . . . 164n4 (chap. 21)
8:9 . . . . 164n4 (chap. 21)
8:11 . . . . 164n4 (chap. 21)
8:20 146
8:21 . . . . 164n4 (chap. 21)
8:29 . . . . 164n4 (chap. 21)
8:31 . . . . 164n4 (chap. 21)
9:1 146
9:13 146
9:14 . . . . 164n4 (chap. 21)
9:20 . . . . 164n4 (chap. 21)
9:30 . . . . 164n4 (chap. 21)
9:34 . . . . 164n4 (chap. 21)
10:1 . . . . 164n4 (chap. 21)
10:3 146
10:6 . . . . 164n4 (chap. 21)
10:7 . . . . 164n4 (chap. 21)
11:3 . . . . 164n4 (chap. 21)

Scripture Index

11:7 44
11:8 . . . . 164n4 (chap. 21)
12 39
12–13 28
12:1–2 45
12:29–30 . . . 43
12:30 . . . . . . 164n4 (chap. 21)
12:35–38 . . . 37
12:38 44
14:4 42
14:5 . . . . 164n4 (chap. 21)
14:19–20 . . . 45
15 . . . . 46, 95
15:1–2 158
15:2–4 45
15:3 95
15:11 45
15:17 54
15:22–17:7 . 48
17:8–16 48
18 128
18:1–27 48
19–20 48
19:4 85
20–40 97
20:2 68
20:2–3 48
21:1–6 49
21:6 49
23:20 127
24 129
24:9–11 . . . . 162n1 (chap. 15)
24:9–18 140
24:11 30
32–34 126
33:12–34:9 . 140
34:1–35 49
34:6 38
40:34 49
40:35 49

Leviticus
book of 50

Numbers
book of 50, 119
9:1–14 50
10:29 158
10:29–36 . . . 50
11:1–30 50
11:31–35 . . . 50
14:1–12 50

14:22 51
16:1–50 50
20:1–13 50
21:21–35 . . . 50
25 . . . . 163n2 (chap. 17)
25:1–18 50
27:17 . . . . . . 163n3

Deuteronomy
book of 50, 120, 127
2:14 129
11:10 108
17:14–17 . . . 103
18:15–19 . . . 141
32 96
32:11 85
32:20 133
34:5 55

Joshua
1–7 53
2 54
4–5 54
5:12 54
5:13–14 56
5:13–15 54
5:14 128
7 96
7:1–26 . . . . . 57, 139
24:15 146
24:29 55

Ruth
book of 83
1:21 84
2:10 86
2:12 . . . . 85, 86
3 87
3:9 86
4:14 86
4:17 86

1 Samuel
book of 88, 89, 97
1–2 92
1–7 88
1:19 89
2:1–10 89
2:8 86
4:3 89
4:8–9 89
5:3 90

5:6 90
5:11 90
5:12 90
6:2 90
6:6 90
6:19–21 90
7:3 91
7:10 91
7:12 91
15 117
17:5 94
17:36 37
18:10–11 . . . 95
19:11–17 . . . 95, 98
21:1–6 95
22:1–5 95
22:11–19 . . . 95
27:1–30:31 . 95

2 Samuel
book of 96, 97
1 95
1:19 95
1:25 95
1:27 95
6:1–19 90
7:12–14 96
15:19–31 . . . 97
16:5–14 97
17 96
17:23 97
19 96
20:9 . . . . 163n2 (chap. 19)
22 96
24 96

1 Kings
book of 104, 105
1–14 . . . . 162n1 (chap. 14)
3 103
6–13 99
6:1 99
6:3 100
6:5 100
6:8 100
7:39 100
8 101
8:56 100
9:15–19 101
9:16 101
9:26 101
10:14–29 . . . 101

174

11:1–8 101
11:14–22. . . 101
11:26–40. . . 101
12:10–11. . . 101
12:28 102
13 . . . . 102, 103
13:2 102
14:1 102
14:20 102
16:33 105
17:17–24. . . 136
18 140
18:41 . . . . . . 162n1 (chap. 15)
22:38 106

2 Kings
book of 104, 105
2 141
5:1–19 136
23:18 103

1 Chronicles
book of 97
21–29. 98

Ezra
book of 116, 117, 119,
             120, 162n2
             (chap. 17),
             163n2 (chap. 17)
9–10. . . . . . . 162n2 (chap. 17)
9:1. . . . . 163n2 (chap. 17)

Nehemiah
book of 116, 117, 119,
             120, 121, 162n2
             (chap. 17),
             163n2 (chap. 17)
9 . . . . 120, 121
10 . . . . 163n2 (chap. 17)
10:30–39. . . 163n2 (chap. 17)
13 . . . . 162n2 (chap.
             17), 163n2
             (chap. 17)
13:25 116

Esther
book of 116, 120
2 117
3:12 118
4:11 118
4:16 118

5:1–3 118
7:1–10 118
9:1–10 118
9:23–38. . . . 118

Job
book of 21

Psalms
7:1. 93
9:15 93
18:2 94
18:11 93
18:12–15. . . 94
19:7–13. . . . 94
20:7–8 94
32:6 93
34:7 93
40:2 93
63:1 94
68:1 94
68:6 94
69:1–2 93
80:8 108
114:3 54
143:8 93

Ecclesiastes
book of 21

Isaiah
book of 112
10–12. 112
24–27. 112
36–37. 113
40–48. 113
48:20 113
49–51. 114
49:15–16. . . 113
51–55. 112
51:9 94
51:9–10. . . . 113
51:12–16. . . 115
52:10 114
52:13 114
53–55. 114
53:1 115
53:2–3. 114
53:5 114
63:11–14. . . 115, 148

Jeremiah
16:14–15. . . 111
31 . . . . 163n1 (chap. 18)
31:33 111

Ezekiel
1 111
1–3. 130
1–24. 112
3 111
4–6 111
9 111
10 111
16 112
20 112
23 112
25–32. 112
29–32. 112
29:3 94
33–48. 112
36–37. 112
40–48. 111
48 111

Daniel
1–5 111

Hosea
11 . . . . 163n1 (chap. 18)
11:1–11. . . . 110

Jonah
4:2. 110

Micah
6:3–5 110
7:15 110
7:18–19. . . . 110

Habakkuk
3 110

Zechariah
10:8–12. . . . 111

Matthew
book of 128, 135
1:14–18. . . . 126
1:21 107
4:4. 157
9:36 . . . . 128, 163n3
10:34 128

175

Scripture Index

26 28
26:27–29 . . . 29
26:29 . . . . . . 31, 156

Mark
1:2 127

Luke
book of 92
1:46–55 89
2:41–50 130
4:24–27 136
7:1–10 136
7:11–17 136
9:30–31 131
9:33 132
9:39 133
9:41 133
17 133
17:22–37 . . . 160n4
22:16 31
22:17 29
22:19 29
24:5–6 135
24:49 98

John
book of 21, 31, 129, 130
2 129
3 129
4 129
5 129
6 129
7 129
8 . . . . 51, 129
8:34 52
8:36 . . . . 16, 52
10 129
12:32 135
18:6 134

Acts
book of 92, 137, 140,
            141
1:1 137
5:1–10 . . . . . 57, 139
5:19 139
9:1–9 140

12 141
12:10 140
22:6–11 140
26:12–18 . . . 140

Romans
book of 144
3:21–26 144
6 146
6:1–14 144
6:2 145
6:15–23 144
7:1–25 144
8 151
8:1–11 144
8:12–17 144
8:18–25 144
8:21 151
8:26–39 144
15:4 14

1 Corinthians
book of 143
3:16–17 143
5:6–8 143
9:10 14
10 . . . . 148, 163n2
            (chap. 17)
10:1 14
10:1–6 14
10:1–13 143
10:2 39
10:11 . . . . . . 14, 143
10:14 145
11:25 156
11:26 156

2 Corinthians
book of 143
3:1–18 144
3:7–18 148
5:1–10 144
6:14 145
6:14–18 144

Galatians
book of 143
3:28 44

4:1–6 143
4:6 143
5:1 . . . . 143, 145
5:16–24 143

Hebrews
book of 148
4 145
11:7 62
13:20–21 . . . 148

1 Peter
3:18–22 63
3:20 63
3:21 64

2 Peter
2:5 62

Jude
5 . . . . 145, 164n3
            (chap. 21)

Revelation
book of 21, 27, 149,
            150, 153, 164n2
            (chap. 22)
1 150
2–3 150
4 150
5 150
7 150
7:14 150
8 150
9–16 150
9:18 . . . . 164n2 (chap. 22)
11 150
12 151
13 150
15 151
15:1 . . . . 164n2 (chap.
            22)
15:3 151
17–18 151
19–20 151
21–22 151
22:20 152